**New Directions for Child and Adolescent Development**

Lene Arnett Jensen
Reed W. Larson
EDITORS-IN-CHIEF

William Damon
FOUNDING EDITOR

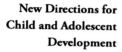

MW01253109

# Rereading Personal Narrative and Life Course

Brian Schiff

EDITOR

Number 145 • Fall 2014
Jossey-Bass
San Francisco

REREADING PERSONAL NARRATIVE AND LIFE COURSE
*Brian Schiff* (ed.)
New Directions for Child and Adolescent Development, no. 145
*Lene Arnett Jensen, Reed W. Larson,* Editors-in-Chief

Microfilm copies of issues and articles are available in 16 mm and 35 mm, as well as microfiche in 105 mm, through University Microfilms, Inc., 300 North Zeeb Road, Ann Arbor, Michigan 48106-1346.

ISSN 1520-3247    electronic ISSN 1534-8687

NEW DIRECTIONS FOR CHILD AND ADOLESCENT DEVELOPMENT is part of The Jossey-Bass Education Series and is published quarterly by Wiley Subscription Services, Inc., a Wiley company, at Jossey-Bass, One Montgomery Street, Suite 1200, San Francisco, CA 94104-4594. Postmaster: Send address changes to New Directions for Child and Adolescent Development, Jossey-Bass, One Montgomery Street, Suite 1200, San Francisco, CA 94104-4594.

*New Directions for Child and Adolescent Development* is indexed in Cambridge Scientific Abstracts (CSA/CIG), CHID: Combined Health Information Database (NIH), Contents Pages in Education (T&F), Educational Research Abstracts Online (T&F), Embase (Elsevier), ERIC Database (Education Resources Information Center), Index Medicus/MEDLINE (NLM), Linguistics & Language Behavior Abstracts (CSA/CIG), Psychological Abstracts/PsycINFO (APA), Social Services Abstracts (CSA/CIG), SocINDEX (EBSCO), and Sociological Abstracts (CSA/CIG).

INDIVIDUAL SUBSCRIPTION RATE (in USD): $89 per year US/Can/Mex, $113 rest of world; institutional subscription rate: $388 US, $428 Can/Mex, $462 rest of world. Single copy rate: $29. Electronic only–all regions: $89 individual, $388 institutional; Print & Electronic–US: $98 individual, $450 institutional; Print & Electronic–Canada/Mexico: $98 individual, $490 institutional; Print & Electronic–Rest of World: $122 individual, $524 institutional.

COVER PHOTOGRAPHS: ©iStock.com/paulaphoto (top); ©iStock.com/vm (middle); ©iStock.com/ericsphotography (bottom)

EDITORIAL CORRESPONDENCE should be e-mailed to the editors-in-chief: Lene Arnett Jensen (ljensen@clarku.edu) and Reed W. Larson (larsonr@illinois.edu).

Jossey-Bass Web address: www.josseybass.com

# CONTENTS

Schiff, B. (2014). Introduction: Development's story in time and place. In B. Schiff (Ed.), *Rereading Personal Narrative and Life Course*. New Directions for Child and Adolescent Development, 145, 1–13.

# 1

# Introduction: Development's Story in Time and Place

*Brian Schiff*

## Abstract

*In this introductory chapter, I place Bertram J. Cohler's (1982) seminal essay* Personal Narrative and Life Course *in the context of the history of narrative psychology and developmental theory. I describe four theses from* Personal Narrative and Life Course, *which impacted developmental theory and research: (a) the self is a narrative project, (b) developmental periods have a distinct narrative character, (c) narratives are always told in (personal and historical) time, and (d) persons strive for coherence. I briefly describe the chapters to follow. However, my main goal is to argue for the implications of narrative for developmental science. Following Cohler, I argue that narrative has a central role to play in understanding human lives and can provide substantial benefit to developmental theory and research. A narrative perspective allows for a complex and nuanced description of developmental phenomena that accounts for the subjective and unpredictable nature of human lives. The narrative interpretation of experience is a primary human activity that alters the meaning of experience and potentially sets development on a new course, rendering the prediction of developmental outcomes a difficult venture. The narrative perspective provides detailed insights into how development unfolds, how persons actually interpret and reinterpret life in time and place, and can help psychologists to engage fundamental questions about the meaning of experience.* © 2014 Wiley Periodicals, Inc.

New Directions for Child and Adolescent Development, no. 145, Fall 2014 © 2014 Wiley Periodicals, Inc.
Published online in Wiley Online Library (wileyonlinelibrary.com). • DOI: 10.1002/cad.20063

Rather than viewing personality development either in terms of continuing stability over time or in terms of a number of well-ordered phases or stages, lives seem to be characterized by often abrupt transformations determined both by expected and eruptive life events and by intrinsic, but not necessarily continuous, developmental factors, including biological aging. These events taking place across the life course are later remembered as elements of a narrative which provides a coherent account of this often disjunctive life course. The form of this narrative is based upon a socially shared belief in Western culture that all narratives, including history, literature, and biographies, must have a beginning, a middle, and an end related to each other in a meaningful manner. (Cohler, 1982, pp. 227–228)

This volume is a reflection on life course developmental theory. In particular, the volume argues for the centrality of narrative interpretation for human development. As a point of departure, we begin from Bertram Joseph Cohler's (1938–2012) seminal contribution to our understanding of developmental psychology. During his prolific career, Cohler published over 200 papers and book chapters. But, Cohler's (1982) chapter *Personal Narrative and Life Course* is clearly one of the most influential. The chapter is one of the first published manuscripts in psychology on the process of storytelling for establishing selfhood and identity and one of the first essays on what would later become narrative psychology. In fact, the chapter was published before Theodore Sarbin (1986) coined the term "narrative psychology" or Jerome Bruner (1990) heralded the "narrative turn in psychology."

Although *Personal Narrative and Life Course* is difficult to locate (PsycInfo doesn't even index the chapter), it has had a substantial impact on how developmental, personality, and clinical psychologists understand identity formation and mental health. But, the chapter can also be viewed as an innovative contribution to developmental theory, an alternative to other perspectives (e.g., biological, cognitive, evolutionary), which argues that development is an interpretative, narrative project.

The formulation, personal narrative and life course, elegantly summarizes three critical developmental processes. First, *personal narrative* captures the fact that persons are engaged in the process of interpretation, often self-interpretation, constantly figuring and refiguring their life and their past into a story of the self through time. Second, *life course* captures the fact that development is not only subjective and individual but also collective and contextual. Persons always find themselves inside a definite horizon of social and cultural conditions, which are historical and changing. Subjective interpretation and contextual forces are essential components for

This volume is dedicated to Bertram Joseph Cohler, a great friend and inspiration.

NEW DIRECTIONS FOR CHILD AND ADOLESCENT DEVELOPMENT • DOI: 10.1002/cad

understanding development's path. But, finally, *putting together personal narrative and life course* highlights the tension between our place in the world and how we make sense of it.

From the first moments of our lives, and even before birth, persons are engaged in the process of making interpretations about life and their place inside it. We need to quickly gather: Whose voice is that? What sounds should I concentrate on? When does a word end? Who are others? What are people talking about? What kind of world do I live in? What are the dangers? What am I? What is a person? What do persons know, think, and feel? What kind of a person am I? What are the goals of life for a person like me? What is the meaning of life? Such facts about the world that we are thrown into are interpretations that each person must make. They are also interpretations that are vital to our survival and well-being.

Of course, newborns are, biologically and socially, prepared for making such interpretations. And, they are not alone in their endeavors. Babies find themselves in sustained interaction with others who are more knowledgeable about the world and its ways and help them to devise provisional answers to these questions and many others (Bruner, 1985; Vygotsky, 1978; Wertsch, 1988). With the support of others, children also learn the forms that persons in their community use to talk about self and others and to express the quality of their experience, intentions, and emotions (Miller, Chen, & Olivarez, Chapter 2 of this volume; Miller & Fung, 2012; Nelson & Fivush, 2004; Wiley, Rose, Burger, & Miller, 1998).

Cohler's great insight, which he developed in numerous publications during his long career, is that storytelling is our way of wrestling with the dilemmas and disruptions that define human existence. Persons make sense of life—of the life that they have, of the life that is given to them. We need to. The challenges are unrelenting, from birth until death. And, the solutions that we arrive at have consequences for our sense of being whole, vital, and progressing toward worthy goals. We advance, or we don't, on the basis of our capacity to create adaptive narratives that make sense to ourselves and to others.

*Personal Narrative and Life Course* was at the avant-garde of the narrative psychology movement, which gained momentum in the late 1980s and 1990s and continues with considerable energy today (Lieblich, Tuval-Mashiach, & Zilber, 1998). Thirty years after its publication, there is now a large literature, from early childhood to old age, on the role of narrative in human development. But, in my opinion, the themes that Cohler advanced in *Personal Narrative and Life Course* are still fresh and future oriented, prescient of an innovative, interpretive, developmental psychology.

## The Self Is a Narrative Project

To readers in 2014, the thesis that self is a narrative project is hardly revolutionary. But, in 1982, it was. Cohler's chapter was published shortly after the 1979 conference *Narrative: The Illusion of Sequence*, organized by W. J. T. Mitchell, and the 1980 publication of a *Critical Inquiry* special issue based upon a selection of conference papers from luminaries such as Hayden White, Roy Schafer, Paul Ricoeur, Jacques Derrida, and Frank Kermode. The special issue, republished soon after (Mitchell, 1981), is regarded as a turning point—when the conversation on narrative became widespread and interdisciplinary (Bruner, 1991a; Hyvärinen, 2006).

However, even in 2014, the implications of a narrative perspective for developmental psychology are yet to be realized. We remain very far away from a developmental psychology that takes meaning and context seriously. It is my hope that this volume of *NDCAD* will serve as a reference point for psychologists who would like to *re*-think their approach to development through the lens of a narrative perspective that is sensitive to interpretation and context in human lives.

For Cohler, narrative is part of the everyday interpretative orientation that humans take in the world. By emphasizing the role of the interpretive process in what Bruner (1991b) would call "self-making," Cohler identified and developed the central tenet of a narrative perspective in psychology—narrative is an interpretative, hermeneutic enterprise (Brockmeier, 2013). Persons are meaning makers engaged in the project of understanding life. Narrative is the means for testing out, fixing, and revising interpretations, for bringing together disparate aspects of our experience and for making self and world comprehensible. Over the course of development, we use narrative in various ways, but beginning in adolescence, we begin to tell stories about our lives, which integrate past experiences with the present and projected future in order to describe a "self" or "identity" (Cohler, 1982; Habermas & Bluck, 2000; Habermas & Hatiboğlu, Chapter 3 of this volume; Habermas & Paha, 2001; McAdams, 1996).

The self becomes a story, an interpretation of our place in the world, which is progressively made and remade over developmental and historical time. Certainly, there is a subjective side to human development in which persons take account of their lives and create themselves, shaping the contours of who they were in the past, who they are now in the present, and what is possible for them in the future. One of the more interesting implications of this argument is that the self is nothing more than an interpretative action (Schiff, 2012). The meanings that persons employ are vitally important in shaping their identity and well-being. In a sense, Cohler's narrative theory radically individualizes the developmental process, making development a personal project that relies heavily on how each person experiences and organizes their past (McAdams, Chapter 5 of this volume).

## Developmental Periods Have a Distinct Narrative Character

Cohler argued that life challenges, adversity and discontinuity, are key moments when narrative is required to reinterpret the past in order to experience a sense of continuity in the face of rupture. Certainly, persons encounter adversity at unique points in their life. Life is full of nonnormative events, which become part of the narrative project and require new interpretations. But, there are also common developmental challenges, both universal and social-cultural, which provide a common narrative character to particular epochs (Hammack & Toolis, Chapter 4 of this volume).

Cohler's work contains a tension between the individualized personal narrative and the normative course of development. Although narrative interpretation provides substantial freedom, understandings are always constrained by biological, cognitive, and social development. Cohler described the transformations in form and content of narratives in three normative developmental transitions (from early childhood to middle childhood, from childhood to adolescence and adulthood, and from adulthood to middle age). Each transformation requires a rebalancing of the person's orientation to the past, present, and future. Cohler (1982) suggested that middle childhood is characterized by turning away from the past, adolescence by "remembering the future" (p. 218), and middle age by a returning concern with the past. Recent work has suggested that early childhood and emerging adulthood are also candidates for life course periods with distinct narrative characters. But, as Lieblich (Chapter 6 of this volume) argues, the character of developmental periods is not uniform or sacrosanct. One of the goals of the chapters collected in this volume is to refine our understanding of narrative across the life course with reference to the emerging scholarly research in this area.

## Narratives Are Always Told in (Personal and Historical) Time

Although biological, cognitive, and social forces may initiate transitions, persons always make sense of these challenges in the context of history, culture, and relationships. In order to understand their lives, persons are always inside a definite temporal and cultural horizon. Persons can only tell a "presently understood" version of the self at a specific moment in developmental time. We can understand the past only through the perspective of the present, an act of narrative reflection or hindsight (Freeman, 2010) in which persons read the past backward through the eyes of later experiences and present circumstances (Schiff & Cohler, 2001).

This presently understood account of self intersects with a specific moment in not only personal history but also world history. Cohler preferred the term "life course" over "life cycle" in order to emphasize development's context and the synergy of personal development with historical, sociological, and cultural circumstances. He was inspired not only by Mannheim's (1928/1952) sociology of generations but also by the innovative work of life course sociologists, such as Neugarten and Elder, who connected historical and social circumstances with subjective experience. Neugarten (1996), Cohler's mentor at The University of Chicago's Committee on Human

Development, argued that persons understand their own development in relationship to socially constructed, but normatively shared, expectations and time tables. For Cohler, Elder's (1974/1999) *Children of the Great Depression* provided solid evidence for Mannheim's thesis that generational cohorts, being similarly "located" in developmental and historical time, share substantial aspects of their mentality while those from previous or later generations experience self and the world differently.

Cohler's conception of personal narrative and life course should also be understood in light of other anti-Piagetian theories of its day in their common effort to move beyond individualistic models of human development, which separate the unfolding of individual development from the social world. Riegel's (1976) notion of dialectics and dialogue in human development and Sameroff and Chandler's (1975) transactional model argue for a dynamic conception of the relationship between persons and the social world, through which, in their exchange, person and world are transformed. Gergen's (1977) aleatoric model argued for the nonuniversal, idiosyncratic, progression of lives over time.

In 1982, Cohler emphasized aspects of historical time in the process of self-interpretation, but it is a short move from history to culture (Cohler, 1992; Cohler & Galatzer-Levy, 2000). Of course, developmental psychology has progressed in the past 30 years. Vygotsky-inspired (Cole, 1996; Holland, Lachicotte, Skinner, & Cain, 1998; Rogoff, 2003) and other cultural conscious theories (LeVine & New, 2008; Stigler, Shweder, & Herdt, 1990) have significantly revised our conception of the universality of human development. There is also a revival of nonlinear theories, including dynamic systems theory, and the continuing influence of transactional models (Sameroff, 2009; van Geert, 2011).

Nevertheless, the notions of personal narrative and life course are still insightful and fresh. Development is never out of context but always inside it. This realization has never been fully appreciated in developmental psychology, which continues to look at itself, deceptively, as generating laws that are true about all humans in all times and all places. Cohler didn't only discuss context but the way that persons make sense of their lives in context. In such a way, he aligned the interpretative capacities of persons with life course theory. Persons are constantly making sense of themselves and the world, in the midst of a changing personal situation and a changing world.

## Persons Strive for Coherence

Although interpretations are forever limited by the present moment, these self-constructions strive for intelligibility on the personal, social, and cultural levels. Narratives should make sense to the teller, capturing the necessary facts about their past. But, stories must also present a followable story to listeners, fulfilling the immediate social and larger cultural expectations of storytelling. Cohler (1982) called this the dual interpretative task, whereby "the account...must be an accurate reflection of the subjectively experienced personal narrative" and it "must do so in a manner which is followable or which makes sense to others" (p. 208). In other words, the personal narrative needs to render the past in a way that is subjectively accurate and makes sense to others to whom we address our stories. We need to answer both the demands of our experience and the demands of the social world to tell our experience cogently.

Finally, Cohler argued that the sense of being coherent through time, narrating a story that successfully brings together past, present, and future, is connected to psychological well-being. In response to ruptures and discontinuities, brought on by a variety of life events, including physical and psychological growth, the personal narrative represents the attempt to maintain a sense of self as continuous, whole, and vital through time. As Cohler (1982) wrote, "transformations are characteristically dramatic and require considerable self-interpretative activity in order to preserve a sense of continuity in the personal narrative which fosters cohesiveness or congruence" (p. 215). The ability to author and reauthor a coherent personal narrative is a characteristic of adaptability—of personal resilience (Cohler, 1987). This is a point that has inspired considerable research in developmental psychology; it also has strong connections with psychoanalytic theorizing, particularly in Self Psychology. As Cohler (1982, 1987) recognized, the sense of coherence communicated in narrative nicely coalesces with Kohut's (1977) contention that the coherence and wholeness of the self are necessary for psychological health, productivity, and vitality. And, "the failure to maintain a coherent life history is characteristic of psychopathology of the self" (Cohler, 1987, p. 400).

## Plan of the Work and Chapter Summary

This volume is authored by Cohler's students, friends, and colleagues. Each in our own way, we were touched by Cohler's scholarship and life. Authors were selected to represent major developmental epochs in narrating the self: childhood (Peggy J. Miller, Eva Chian-Hui Chen, & Megan Olivarez, Chapter 2), adolescence (Tilmann Habermas & Neşe Hatiboğlu, Chapter 3), emerging adulthood (Phillip L. Hammack & Erin Toolis, Chapter 4), middle age (Dan P. McAdams, Chapter 5), and old age (Amia Lieblich, Chapter 6). Authors were also asked to address one or more of the central theses that Cohler argued in his 1982 chapter and outlined above: (a) *the self is a narrative project*, (b) *developmental periods have a distinct narrative character*, (c) *narratives are always told in (personal and historical) time*, and (d) *persons strive for coherence*. Mark Freeman was asked to write an epilogue and comment on the chapters.

Read together, the chapters form a larger description of narrative's origins in conversation and the various uses that narrative is put to over

NEW DIRECTIONS FOR CHILD AND ADOLESCENT DEVELOPMENT • DOI: 10.1002/cad

developmental time. Miller, Chen, and Olivarez (Chapter 2) argue that the personal narrative has its beginnings in early childhood's stories of personal experience, in which specific episodes of recent experience are jointly told and scaffold children's emerging understanding of what it means to be a self over time and within a particular cultural world. Habermas and Hatiboğlu (Chapter 3) argue that adolescents begin to draw in larger segments of time and sweeping themes about the self, provocatively suggesting that contextual coherence, seeing the place of the self in history and culture, is a feature of adolescent narratives. Hammack and Toolis (Chapter 4) argue that the functions and themes of narrating in adulthood display a greater openness than adolescence; through the activity of narrative engagement, persons negotiate an individual conception of adulthood that responds to socially and culturally imagined master narratives of adulthood. In middle adulthood, McAdams (Chapter 5) argues that narratives respond to the developmental challenge to view life as purposeful and the projects of adulthood as having a larger meaning. Although the notion of purpose in life could be variously conceived in different cultural settings, in American history, folklore and media, the redemptive narrative is especially well articulated and conceived for sustaining generative projects. In old age, Amia Lieblich (Chapter 6) questions the ubiquity of reviewing the past for the construction of a coherent personal narrative as a requisite for positive aging. Lieblich argues that social and cultural contexts need to be considered as motivating forces for engagement with the past or other strategies for managing identity in old age. Finally, Mark Freeman (Chapter 7) provides critical insights into the nature of narrative over the life course and the legacy of Cohler's work.

## Development's Story in Context

Although celebrating Cohler's scholarship and the research that it inspired is a worthy goal, this volume is essentially concerned with the future direction of developmental psychology. What is the legacy of these ideas for a more complex, and more realistic, understanding of developmental process? Or, why should developmental psychology take narrative seriously?

Following Cohler, I believe that narrative has a central role to play in understanding human lives and can provide substantial benefit to developmental theory and research. Human development is not only about objective circumstances that can be reliably measured and quantified in variables but it is equally about how persons interpret themselves and the world around them. Variable-centered research is important and complementary, but it conceals central aspects of human development. A narrative perspective can contribute to the project of developmental psychology by revealing the interpretative processes in which persons make connections between actions, experiences, and emotions. Narrative provides the tools to understand how people make sense of life, self, and world, and the consequences of meaning making.

This descriptive research activity of apprehending, in a more grounded and realistic light, what happens during development is a critical contribution in and of itself. Indeed, one way of viewing the significance of narrative for developmental psychology is fulfilling the goal of describing, and understanding, the phenomenon of development itself. The longstanding orientation toward understanding, *verstehen*, found in the writings of Max Weber, Wilhelm Dilthey, and Cohler's mentor, Gordon Allport, argues that the aim of the human sciences is to make intelligible, and knowable, the subjective bases of lived experience and the meaning of experience. Following in this tradition, narrative aspires to the epistemological goal of understanding, in contrast to the goal of prediction that underlies the vast majority of research in psychology and the social sciences.

Narrative offers developmental psychologists a window into the complexity of human lives, to comprehend the way that persons grow into meanings, how subjective construals of self and the world emerge over time, in conversation with significant others and under the sway of historical and cultural currents. By paying close attention to how persons interpret themselves, others, and the world, a narrative perspective allows for a nuanced description of developmental phenomena that accounts for the subjective experience of what life is like and what it means to me. But, this is just the beginning of the story. Narrative's insight into subjectivity helps us to understand several persistent lacunae in developmental knowledge.

First, narrative interpretation inserts a wild card in human development. Persons are actors in the creation of their own development, active in making interpretations, and then altering and revising the meaning of experience. This interpretative activity always has the potential to *re*-set development on a new course, rendering the orderly prediction of developmental outcomes a difficult, if not impossible, venture. Psychology continues to be plagued with questions about the predictive power of our analyses in which large portions of the data are left unaccounted for by our statistical models. What doesn't fit into our predictive equations, we label error variance. But, of course, error suggests that our models need to be rethought, and I believe expanded to incorporate the complex and particular manner by which persons "make life" and "make self." The solution is not better statistical models but complementary approaches that can account for human interpretation, which, in my estimation, is one of the major reasons why human lives are so uncertain but also so fascinating.

I am not suggesting that statistical models are not useful or worthy of our time and energy, but rather they can't account for all developmental phenomena. The interpretative, day in and day out recasting of experience, capitalizes on the possible and virtually ensures the unpredictability of outcomes. The narrative perspective is sensitive to these interpretative twists and turns, providing detailed insights into how development unfolds and how experiences are constantly reworked in order to arrive at outcomes that are unforeseeable. As Cohler (1982) argued, "the interpretative or narrative

NEW DIRECTIONS FOR CHILD AND ADOLESCENT DEVELOPMENT • DOI: 10.1002/cad

approach is based on an assumption that lives change over time in ways not necessarily predictable" (p. 210). Once again, following Gergen's (1977) "aleatoric" model, Cohler (1982) wrote that "the course of life may be better understood as a series of . . . marked discontinuities in development, rather than as transformations in which later phases appear to emerge from earlier ones" (p. 214). Michael Lewis (1997), summarizing his views on short-term and long-term longitudinal research, has argued that "the best that can be said is that there sometimes is very limited support for the belief that earlier events are connected to later ones" (p. 52). The nonlinearity of human lives is due not only to chance events but also to the influence of interpretative activity, which has the ability to reimagine the past and present and set the future on a new path. Only by looking closely at how persons interpret their lives over time can we arrive at a more complete account of the capriciousness so characteristic of human lives.

Second, narrative is able to "personalize" developmental knowledge. As a part of psychological science, developmental psychology strives to account for generalizations beyond the persons being studied. But, we mistake "knowledge of the average" for "knowledge of the general" (Bakan, 1966; Lamiell, 2003). We aggregate information across a wide number of cases and analyze the means from these data, which we assume describe something real, in general, about individual trajectories. In a chapter aptly titled *Missing Persons*, Elliot Mishler (1996) argues that aggregation conceals the fact that advances and setbacks to developmental ends are part and parcel of any developmental process, including basic ones like cognitive, emotional, or identity development. We take the means from aggregated data and mistake the aggregates for individual developmental markers. The result is that development looks much more orderly, steplike, and linear than it actually is. Indeed, as we all know from our life experience, there are a great number of pathways to reach any developmental goal. And, when we start to investigate how persons interpret themselves and their past, we understand that advances, setbacks, lapses, and gaps are all a part of the developmental process. Life is much more messy and persons much more inconsistent than aggregated data allow us to imagine.

Although research remains on the level of the group average, there is no clear formula for applying knowledge derived from statistical aggregates to individual persons. Our aggregated data and statistical analyses translate badly back to persons. Sometimes the data do seem to help us understand the person sitting in front of us at the dinner table, the client in our clinical practice, or the person on the street. But, just as often, what the data mean for *this* person is limited and opaque. How does one translate averages back to a person?

When the numbers can't account for diversity in developmental trajectories, we are often left with the well-worn saw, "everyone is different." Although this is undoubtedly true, a narrative perspective can help us to move beyond an empty account of difference through the systematic description of *how* and *why* differences are realized. Building theories from detailed observations of how persons interpret self and world, narrative perspectives document the variety of lifeways through development and provide insight into how interpretative strategies of reflecting on experience (Freeman, 2006) and positioning the self in conversation (Bamberg, 2004) shape the course of development.

Finally, narrative deserves a special place in developmental psychology because narrative interpretation is key to understanding basic problems in human development about how persons grow into meaning in order to *make life* and *make self*. As Cohler argued, we need to put this interpretative capacity in its correct context. Interpretation is personal but it is also temporal and social; development's story is always situated, interpretation is fused with the sights, sounds, smells, and feelings of a particular time and place, at a definite stage in development and life experience, which is likewise situated in a conversational setting and in a cultural and historical horizon of meaning. In narrative, we come to understand persons, as who they are, as individuals with a particular life experience, making interpretations, imagining, and inhabiting notions about self and life. Such a thick picture of development is critical for advancing the project of understanding human beings and how our interpretative capacity works to cobble together a version of self, life, and world.

## References

Bakan, D. (1966). The test of significance in psychological research. *Psychological Bulletin, 66*(6), 423–437.

Bamberg, M. (2004). 'We are young, responsible and male': Form and functions of 'slut bashing' in male identity constructions in 15-year-olds. *Human Development, 47*(6), 331–353.

Brockmeier, J. (2013). Fact and fiction: Exploring the narrative mind. In M. Hatavara, L.-C. Hydén, & M. Hyvärinen (Eds.), *The travelling concepts of narrative* (pp. 121–140). Philadelphia, PA: John Benjamins.

Bruner, J. (1985). *Child's talk: Learning to use language.* New York, NY: W. W. Norton.

Bruner, J. (1990). *Acts of meaning.* Cambridge, MA: Harvard University Press.

Bruner, J. (1991a). The narrative construction of reality. *Critical Inquiry, 18*, 1–21.

Bruner, J. (1991b). Self-making and world-making. *Journal of Aesthetic Education, 25*(1), 67–78.

Cohler, B. J. (1982). Personal narrative and life course. In P. Baltes & O. G. Brim (Eds.), *Life span development and behavior* (Vol. 4, pp. 205–241). New York, NY: Academic Press.

Cohler, B. J. (1987). Adversity, resilience, and the study of lives. In E. J. Anthony & B. J. Cohler (Eds.), *The invulnerable child* (pp. 363–424). New York, NY: The Guilford Press.

Cohler, B. J. (1992). Intent and meaning in psychoanalysis and cultural study. In T. Schwartz, G. M. White, & C. A. Lutz (Eds.), *New directions in psychological anthropology* (pp. 269–293). Cambridge, UK: Cambridge University Press.

Cohler, B. J., & Galatzer-Levy, R. M. (2000). *The course of gay and lesbian lives: Social and psychoanalytic perspectives.* Chicago, IL: The University of Chicago Press.

Cole, M. (1996). *Cultural psychology: A once and future discipline.* Cambridge, MA: Harvard University Press.

Elder, G. H., Jr. (1974/1999). *Children of the great depression: Social change in life experience* (25th anniversary ed.). Boulder, CO: Westview Press.

Freeman, M. (2006). Life "on holiday"?: In defense of big stories. *Narrative Inquiry, 16*(1), 131–138.

Freeman, M. (2010). *Hindsight: The promise and peril of looking backward.* New York, NY: Oxford University Press.

Gergen, K. J. (1977). Stability, change and chance in understanding human development. In N. Datan & H. Rheese (Eds.), *Life span developmental psychology, dialectic perspectives* (pp. 135–157). New York, NY: Academic Press.

Habermas, T., & Bluck, S. (2000). Getting a life: The emergence of the life story in adolescence. *Psychological Bulletin, 126*(5), 748–769.

Habermas, T., & Paha, C. (2001). The development of coherence in adolescent's life narratives. *Narrative Inquiry, 11*(1), 35–54.

Holland, D., Lachicotte, W., Jr., Skinner, D., & Cain, C. (1998). *Identity and agency in cultural worlds.* Cambridge, MA: Harvard University Press.

Hyvärinen, M. (2006). Towards a conceptual history of narrative. In M. Hyvärinen, A. Korhonen, & J. Mykkänen (Eds.), *The travelling concept of narrative* (pp. 20–41). Retrieved from https://helda.helsinki.fi/handle/10138/25742

Kohut, H. (1977). *The restoration of the self.* Chicago, IL: The University of Chicago Press.

Lamiell, J. T. (2003). *Beyond individual and group differences: Human individuality, scientific psychology, and William Stern's critical personalism.* Thousand Oaks, CA: Sage.

LeVine, R. A., & New, R. S. (Eds.). (2008). *Anthropology and child development: A cross-cultural reader.* Malden, MA: Blackwell.

Lewis, M. (1997). *Altering fate: Why the past does not predict the future.* New York, NY: The Guilford Press.

Lieblich, A., Tuval-Mashiach, R., & Zilber, T. (1998). *Narrative research: Reading, analysis, and interpretation.* Thousand Oaks, CA: Sage.

Mannheim, K. (1928/1952). The problem of generations. In P. Kecskemeti (Ed. & Trans.), *Essays on the sociology of knowledge* (pp. 276–322). New York, NY: Routledge.

McAdams, D. P. (1996). Personality, modernity, and the storied self: A contemporary framework for studying persons. *Psychological Inquiry, 7*(4), 295–321.

Miller, P. J., & Fung, H. (2012). How socialization happens on the ground: Narrative practices as alternate socializing pathways in Taiwanese and European-American families: I. Introduction. *Monographs of the Society for Research in Child Development, 77*(1), 1–14.

Mishler, E. G. (1996). Missing persons: Recovering developmental stories/histories. In R. Jessor, A. Colby, & R. A. Shweder (Eds.), *Ethnography and human development: Context and meaning in social inquiry* (pp. 73–99). Chicago, IL: The University of Chicago Press.

Mitchell, W. J. T. (Ed.). (1981). *On narrative.* Chicago, IL: The University of Chicago Press.

Nelson, K., & Fivush, R. (2004). The emergence of autobiographical memory: A social cultural developmental theory. *Psychological Review, 111*(2), 486–511.

Neugarten, B. L. (1996). *The meanings of age: Selected papers of Bernice L. Neugarten.* Chicago, IL: The University of Chicago Press.

Riegel, K. F. (1976). The dialectics of human development. *American Psychologist, 31*(10), 689–700.

Rogoff, B. (2003). *The cultural nature of human development.* New York, NY: Oxford University Press.

Sameroff, A. J. (Ed.). (2009). *The transactional model of development: How children and contexts shape each other*. Washington, DC: American Psychological Association Press.

Sameroff, A. J., & Chandler, M. (1975). Reproductive risk and the continuum of caretaking casualty. In F. D. Horowitz, M. Hetherington, S. Scarr-Salapatek, & G. Sigel (Eds.), *Review of child development research* (Vol. 4, pp. 187–244). Chicago, IL: University of Chicago Press.

Sarbin, T. R. (1986). The narrative as a root metaphor for psychology. In T. R. Sarbin (Ed.), *Narrative psychology: The storied nature of human conduct* (pp. 3–21). Westport, CT: Praeger.

Schiff, B. (2012). The function of narrative: Toward a narrative psychology of meaning. *Narrative Works: Issues, Investigations & Interventions*, 2(1), 34–47.

Schiff, B., & Cohler, B. (2001). Telling survival backward: Holocaust survivors narrate the past. In G. M. Kenyon, P. G. Clark, & B. de Vries (Eds.), *Narrative gerontology: Theory, research and practice* (pp. 113–136). New York, NY: Springer.

Stigler, J. W., Shweder, R. A., & Herdt, G. (Eds.). (1990). *Cultural psychology: Essays on comparative human development*. New York, NY: Cambridge University Press.

van Geert, P. (2011). The contribution of complex dynamic systems to development. *Child Development Perspectives*, 5(4), 273–278.

Vygotsky, L. S. (1978). *Mind in society: The development of higher psychological processes*. Cambridge, MA: Harvard University Press.

Wertsch, J. V. (1988). *Vygotsky and the social formation of mind*. Cambridge, MA: Harvard University Press.

Wiley, A. R., Rose, A. J., Burger, L. K., & Miller, P. J. (1998). Constructing autonomous selves through narrative practices: A comparative study of working-class and middle-class families. *Child Development*, 69(3), 833–847.

BRIAN SCHIFF *is an associate professor and the chair of the Department of Psychology at the American University of Paris.*

Miller, P. J., Chen, E. C.-H., & Olivarez, M. (2014). Narrative making and remaking in the early years: Prelude to the personal narrative. In B. Schiff (Ed.), *Rereading Personal Narrative and Life Course. New Directions for Child and Adolescent Development, 145,* 15–27.

2

# Narrative Making and Remaking in the Early Years: Prelude to the Personal Narrative

*Peggy J. Miller, Eva Chian-Hui Chen, Megan Olivarez*

## Abstract

*Although very young children are unable to formulate a personal narrative of the life course, their everyday lives are steeped in narratives. Drawing on ethnographic studies in diverse sociocultural worlds, we argue that the early years of life form a vital preamble to the personal narrative. In this phase of life, the universal predisposition to narrative takes root and burgeons as young children step into whichever narrative practices are at hand, practices that are culturally differentiated from the beginning. As children narrate their experiences, they orient themselves in time and establish the interpretive grounds for intelligibility. This process is highly dynamic. Stories recur, stories are repeated, stories are revamped, and stories disappear. These dynamics constitute, for many children, an intense narrative initiation that defines early childhood as a developmental context. By the end of early childhood, they are well versed in making and remaking narratives and show an incipient ability to open a wider temporal window on their own experience. © 2014 Wiley Periodicals, Inc.*

W hen do individuals begin to construct a personal narrative of the life course? In his seminal essay, Bertram Cohler (1982) does not address this question directly. However, he does acknowledge that something momentous happens in adolescence. New capacities for reflective thought and for perceiving temporal continuity emerge. Cohler argues that these developments, along with the formation of identity in the Eriksonian sense, make it possible for adolescents to create a coherent narrative of the self over the long term. Charlotte Linde (1989), whose linguistic analysis of the "life story" complements Cohler's psychological account, makes a similar point. She argues that stories that become part of the life story begin to develop in early adolescence in concert with the development of a distinct sense of social identity.

We do not take issue with the idea that adolescence marks a watershed in the development of the personal narrative (see Habermas & Hatiboğlu, Chapter 3 of this volume; McAdams, Chapter 5 of this volume). We claim, however, that the origins of the personal narrative can be traced to a much earlier moment in development. In this chapter, we draw on research on young children's everyday participation in narrative practices to argue that the early years of life form a vital preamble to the personal narrative, as Cohler envisioned it. In the first two sections of the chapter, we discuss threads of continuity between children's early experience of narrative and the personal narrative. These threads pertain to Cohler's theses that the self is a narrative project and that persons strive for coherence, respectively. In the third section, we turn to Cohler's temporality thesis. We argue that there is a pronounced discontinuity between early narrative, with its limited temporal horizon, and the personal narrative, which embraces multiple temporal perspectives from the past, the present, and the future. We also consider the earliest roots of an expanded temporal horizon. In the fourth section, we address perhaps the most profound and original of Cohler's insights, namely, the dynamic nature of the personal narrative, its constant revisability. This, we argue, may be the strongest continuity with early narrative. In early childhood, stories recur, stories are repeated, stories are revamped, and stories disappear. These dynamics are part and parcel of the intense narrative initiation that defines early childhood as a developmental context. By the end of early childhood, children are already well versed in making and remaking narratives of their own experiences. We conclude with some suggestions for future research.

## Stories of Personal Experience: An Early Bridge to the Personal Narrative

In *Acts of Meaning*, Jerome Bruner (1990) argued that young human beings come into the world equipped with a predisposition for narrative that allows them to quickly grasp and use the narrative resources that they encounter. He argued further that this preparedness for narrative takes root

NEW DIRECTIONS FOR CHILD AND ADOLESCENT DEVELOPMENT • DOI: 10.1002/cad

and burgeons in the normative social practices of telling and interpreting into which the child is born. By this account, children who will consciously fashion personal narratives in the teen years are already avidly consuming narratives and making meaning before they enter preschool. Research on young children from a variety of cultural and socioeconomic backgrounds supports this account and reveals that youngsters' precocious affinity for narrative dovetails with their families' vigorous efforts, witting and unwitting, to immerse them in a world of narratives (e.g., Engel, 1995; Miller, Koven, & Lin, 2011; Miller & Sperry, 2012; Nelson, 1989, 1996; Ochs & Capps, 2001).

In piecing together threads of continuity between early development and the emergence of the personal narrative of the individual's life over the long term, one particular genre, stories of personal experience, serves as an obvious bridge. This is especially apparent with respect to Cohler's thesis that the self is a narrative project. Like the genre that he called the personal narrative, stories of personal experience are self-constructions told in the first person; the storyteller and the story protagonist are one and the same. Yet these two autobiographical genres are very different in scope. The personal narrative is like a serialized book-length autobiography, whereas personal stories are like narrative snapshots of the self. Complicating matters, these genres have tended to attract scholars from disciplines that do not usually converse with one another, with psychologists gravitating to the personal narrative and sociolinguists and folklorists to stories of personal experience. This disciplinary partitioning may help to explain the confusing terminological overlap (*the personal narrative* vs. *stories of personal experience*).

The classic paper on stories of personal experience was written by sociolinguists William Labov and Joshua Waletzky (1967) who collected a large corpus of such stories while recording the vernacular speech of ordinary Americans.[1] They defined stories of personal experience as oral accounts, told in conversation in which the narrator evokes a particular past event from his or her experience; the account is temporally ordered and conveys the point or significance of the story (see Bamberg's 1997 special issue of the *Journal of Narrative and Life History*, which addresses the influential afterlife of this foundational work). Although stories of personal experience can be set in a variety of time frames, most research has continued to focus on stories of particular past events.

Unlike the personal narrative (Cruikshank, 1990; Linde, 1989), stories of personal experience are a cultural universal (Miller & Moore, 1989). And they count as a "primary" genre in the Baktinian sense, combining readily to form more complex "secondary" genres (Miller, Hengst, Alexander, & Sperry, 2000; Ochs & Capps, 2001). This property of stories of personal experience is critical to our argument that this genre serves as a bridge to the personal narrative: stories of personal experience supply the raw material that people use in devising accounts of their lives over the long term (Linde,

1989). Individuals select, revise, and delete stories; juxtapose and reorder stories relative to one another; and recalibrate the meaning of stories in a process of continual reconstruction. In this process, only a fraction of the stories of personal experience that the individual has told over the course of his or her life will end up in the life story.

Stories of personal experience not only furnish the components of the life story but they also emerge early in development, providing a developmental bridge to the life story. By roughly two years of age children are able to participate in telling stories of their own past experiences in interaction with family members. For example, a 28-month-old child and her mother conarrated a recent visit to the Baltimore aquarium: when the mother asked, "Did we go down to see the fishes?" the child nodded, gazing intently at her mother. Then, speaking in an excited tone of voice, she said, "I see big fish." The two then proceeded to talk about the lobsters. A month later, this same child told family members, "Jimmy pinched my fingernail. I was crying" (Miller & Sperry, 1988). In other stories recorded in socioculturally diverse families within and beyond the United States, small narrators related mishaps (falling down, getting hurt while sledding), frightening experiences (a ride at an amusement park, a movie that made the narrator flee from the scene), misdeeds (writing on the wall, crying inappropriately), achievements (helping to cook, mastering a puzzle), and other noteworthy events (Miller, Cho, & Bracey, 2005; Miller, Fung, Lin, Chen, & Boldt, 2012). As these examples illustrate, very young children's stories are simple, invoking departures from the baseline of their ordinary, expectable experience. These perturbations have emotional and moral import to the child and his significant others. Already, only a few years into the life course, self making is demonstrably a narrative project: youngsters use first-person stories to register and make sense of disjunctions in their own experience.

## Rendering Personal Experience Intelligible

From the beginning, children's partners in this endeavor—parents and other family members—engage them in narrative practices that are culturally loaded. When children first encounter personal storytelling, they do not encounter a neutral medium into which cultural values are later injected. There is now a sizeable body of work that shows that personal storytelling is culturally differentiated from the beginning (Miller et al., 2011), encompassing multiple dimensions of variability (Miller & Moore, 1989; Ochs & Capps, 2001). Whether personal storytelling is highly valued, what counts as a reportable event, how much fictionalization is allowed, which participant roles are favored—all of these and many other features are subject to variation.

One dimension of variation is especially relevant to Cohler's thesis that personal narratives strive for intelligibility. In our comparative work,

NEW DIRECTIONS FOR CHILD AND ADOLESCENT DEVELOPMENT • DOI: 10.1002/cad

we found that stories of personal experience carry culturally divergent interpretive frameworks. For example, children in European-American working-class communities in Baltimore and Chicago told and listened to a version of personal storytelling that privileged linearly sequenced, highly coherent accounts of literally true events, susceptible to framing as verbal art. Although many kinds of experiences could be rendered intelligible within these interpretive parameters, narrators in these communities often exploited the dramatic potential of the genre to project tough, assertive selves who faced harsh realities, stood up for themselves, and defended their rights and their dignity (Miller et al., 2005). By contrast, their middle-class counterparts in another community in Chicago encountered a child-affirming interpretive framework that downplayed their misdeeds and shortcomings, in deference to their psychological vulnerability and need for high self-esteem (Miller et al., 2005). Comparisons of these children with middle-class Chinese children in Taipei, Taiwan, revealed yet another interpretive framework. The Taipei children and their parents used personal storytelling didactically, treating young children's past misdeeds as highly reportable for their pedagogical value (Miller et al., 2012). Parents narrated children's transgressions at length, debriefed the child about the negative consequences of his actions, explained the impact on his parents and others, urged amendments, and encouraged listening and reflection.

Each of these culturally salient interpretive frameworks offered young children a different set of normative resources for making sense of their own experiences and for rendering them intelligible to others. These frameworks were repeatedly applied to the child's own past experience by children themselves in active connivance with the most important people in their lives. Each didactic story (in Taipei) or affirming story (in Chicago) provided another opportunity for children to hear which of their experiences were reportable, how their actions and feelings were temporally and causally related, and how their actions should be evaluated. In this way, interpretive biases were not only reproduced but also repeatedly instantiated in personally relevant terms.

We argue that children's active engagement with these routine practices creates the interpretive ground on which they come to understand themselves in this way or that: as alert to their own failings but capable of improvement, for example, or as alert to their own strengths and needing to express themselves. Because young children have limited awareness of their own and others' actions and because the practices that instantiate these cultural slants recur habitually, this early moment in the cocreation of selves and cultures helps to explain how habitus gets established (Bourdieu, 1990): particular interpretive biases come to be deeply taken for granted, inducing a kind of social "unconsciousness." Years later, when these same children begin to craft personal narratives that are intelligible to self and others, some interpretive strategies will feel "natural," "plausible," and

NEW DIRECTIONS FOR CHILD AND ADOLESCENT DEVELOPMENT • DOI: 10.1002/cad

self-evidently "right" while others will not. Indeed, some strategies may be unimaginable.

## Expanding Temporal Horizons

Every account of narrative treats temporality as a defining feature, and Cohler's account is no exception. The personal narrative is a narrative of the individual's life over the long term, connecting past, present, and future. This kind of sense making is not available to the very young because their temporal horizon is limited both by their life experience and their immature cognitive capacities. It is not the case, however, that young children have no temporal horizon: as personal storytelling illustrates, they are not confined entirely to the here and now. When Yoyo, a 3,6-year-old from Taipei, launched a story by saying, "I released two birds yesterday," he operated with two temporal vantage points, one of which he specified explicitly, using a temporal adverb. The narrating self told the story in the present moment, invoking the actions of the self-protagonist at an earlier moment in time. This kind of temporal coordination enacts self-continuity over a brief temporal interval, the period between an event that the child experienced the day before and the child's here-and-now telling of that event.

When do children begin to use narrative to explore a more extended metric of the self over time? As far as we know, there is little research on this question although there are linguistic studies of older children's developing mastery of temporal markers (see, e.g., Chang, 2004; Pathman, Doydum, & Bauer, 2013; Peterson, Wang, & Hou, 2009; Wang, Peterson, & Hou, 2010). To explore this question, we conducted a preliminary analysis of temporal comparisons in a large sample of stories of personal experience, encompassing the period from 2,6 to 4 years of age.[2] We found that the child protagonist was portrayed as changing over time in roughly 0.06 of the stories.[3] For example, one story from our middle-class Chicago sample revealed that Patrick (4,0) used to hang from the pipes in the basement but his mother told him that water would come out; now he knows better and no longer hangs from the pipes. In this example, the narrating participants used the verb "used to" to contrast Patrick's habitual behavior at an earlier time in his life to his habitual behavior now, in the ongoing present.

In some cases, child narrators even used conventional labels ("baby," "little kid," "big") or age markers to chart their progress along a normative life course. For example, when the researcher asked Karen (3,6), a child from the same Chicago neighborhood, how she learned to do puzzles so well, Karen said, "When I was a baby I didn't know how," leading the researcher to say, "You're getting big, aren't you? What else can you do now that you couldn't do when you were a baby?" Karen replied, "I can do everything," and proceeded to demonstrate hopping on one foot. She added, "Katie can't do that 'cause she still wears diapers." Later in the conversation, Karen returned to the topic of herself as a baby:

Karen: I, I weared diapers before (laughs)

Researcher: You wore diapers before?

Karen: When I was a baby.

Researcher: Um hum.

Karen: I used to wear diapers.

Researcher: And what else when you were a baby? What did you drink out of?

After further discussion of what she could and couldn't do when she was a baby, Karen said, "When I was growing up, I had my birthday." This example suggests that Karen understood herself to be a growing person, who had once been a baby but who has now advanced far beyond the limitations of babyhood. Unlike the stories of personal experience discussed above, in which the narrator referenced a single past event, Karen's story conveys a somewhat different sense of herself over time, a recognition that her experience can be divided into extended temporal intervals that are distinct and ordered (when she was a baby vs. now, when she is big). She seems to be striving to do what Freeman (Chapter 7 of this volume) calls "looking backward." In addition, Karen seems to understand that babyhood, with its characteristic behaviors (wearing diapers, drinking from a bottle, not being able to walk or hop on one foot), transcends her own experience: Katie, who is a baby, cannot hop on one foot just as Karen could not when she was a baby. The temporal window is widening and a normative life course is getting plotted. Not only that: a distinct, buoyant voice can be heard, "I can do everything. I can hop on one foot. Wanna see?"

## Narrative Dynamics

Cohler's understanding of temporality was complex and subtle, going far beyond the idea that the personal narrative connects past, present, and future. He emphasized that the project of constructing a personal narrative is never finished: individuals narrate their lives time and time again. They successively revisit and reformulate their interpretations, seeking to make sense of their lives in the face of change, both anticipated discontinuities and unanticipated contingencies. And these repeated narrative excursions are themselves embedded in multiple temporal trajectories: the history of particular relationships, the disjunctions of the normative life course, and the macrohistorical moment in which all of these other trajectories unfold.

We suggest that Cohler's understanding of the dynamics of the personal narrative *in* time is his most profound and original insight, an insight whose

NEW DIRECTIONS FOR CHILD AND ADOLESCENT DEVELOPMENT • DOI: 10.1002/cad

full import has yet to be fully exploited in psychological research. We argue further that the dynamic nature of narrative as an everyday practice is one of the strongest threads of continuity between the personal narrative and early development. As a developmental context, early childhood is first and foremost a period of intense narrative initiation. When families immerse young children in a world of stories, children not only learn to evoke their past experiences in the present moment, aligning past and present selves, but they also experience again and again that stories unfold in real time.

Readers who are unfamiliar with the ethnographic literature may be surprised to learn just how frequently stories arise in everyday family life. For example, in our comparative study of middle-class European-American families in Chicago and middle-class Chinese families in Taipei, personal storytelling occurred four to five times per hour on average in both sites (Miller et al., 2012). Not only were the rates remarkably similar, but they were also remarkably stable over time in this longitudinal study: personal storytelling continued apace at 2,6; 3,0; 3,6; and 4,0 years of age. This similarity coexisted with striking cultural differences in interpretive frameworks (described earlier) and participant roles, creating distinct developmental pathways for the Chicago and Taipei children. The steady recurrence, hour after hour, day after day, of these culturally saturated stories afforded children an enormous number of opportunities to render their own experiences intelligible in local terms.

We have already mentioned one theoretical implication of the sheer frequency of recurring stories of personal experience early in life, namely, the creation of habitus (Bourdieu, 1990). Sociocultural theory points to another: it posits that as children accrue more and more experience in discourse-mediated social interactions, they become more sophisticated users of those discursive tools, first on the social plane and later on the psychological plane (Holland, Lachicotte, Skinner, & Cain, 1998; Miller, Fung, & Mintz, 1996; Nelson, 1996; Scribner & Cole, 1981; Wertsch, 1991). This suggests that young children's immersion in personal storytelling helps to explain how this practice infiltrates their hearts and minds, becoming a means by which they render themselves intelligible to themselves and others.

Both of these theoretical perspectives highlight the redundancy inherent in routine practices. But this is only one side of the coin. It is important to acknowledge that personal storytelling is a situated *social* practice (Hammack & Toolis, Chapter 4 of this volume); as such, it is inherently variable, reflecting the specific contexts in which stories are told and received (Habermas & Hatiboğlu, Chapter 3 of this volume). Tellers and listeners appropriate and alter normative interpretive frameworks while creating and responding to here-and-now social contingencies. After declaring, "I released two birds yesterday," Yoyo went on to explain that his action was accidental, a claim that his mother accepted but his older brother disputed. In the course of a single conarration, Yoyo encountered two different perspectives on his past actions, one of which required that he defend his version of what happened. This example illustrates that young children's participation in personal storytelling is not fixed or mechanical but flexible.

It also shows that children's early experience of narrative offers lessons in a fundamental property of narrative making and remaking: experience can be narrated from different perspectives. This lesson is most powerfully conveyed in repetitions of the "same" story. In every community that we have studied, we find that recurrence of culturally inflected stories forms the baseline of narrative practice, but within that baseline, families single out particular past events to revisit again and again (Miller, 1994; Miller et al., 2012).

For example, Karen (4,0) participated in multiple stories about her intense attachment to her special blanket and her struggle to relinquish it, an early experience of the kind of challenge that impels narrative reinterpretation (Cohler, 1982; Schiff, Chapter 1 of this volume). In one story, Karen related that she tried to give up her blanket when visiting her grandfather but couldn't stop dreaming about it. Immediately after this conarration, Karen's father retold the story, with Karen as bystander, adding details that Karen had not included, " . . . Karen says, 'I don't need this anymore,' and she walked over and threw it in the garbage can. I said, 'That's cool.'" Later in this same observation, Karen and her mother returned to the topic of Karen's blanket. Karen insisted that she would not give up her blanket and then she and her mother reminisced about her first special blanket, a teddy bear blanket from infancy. They then renarrated the incident in which Karen tried to give up her blanket but kept dreaming about it. Her mother asked, "Did you miss it? I bet you did and said, 'Where is my blankey?' [said tearfully]." Karen replied, "I kept dreaming about it," and the conarration continued. Unlike Karen's father, whose account encouraged Karen to give up the blanket, Karen's mother conveyed via words and voice quality, the sadness that she imagined Karen felt, her sense of loss about the missing "blankey." This affectively charged diminutive from the family's lexicon of baby talk harkens back to babyhood and perhaps to the teddy bear blanket that the two had discussed moments earlier.

Didi, a child from Taipei, provides another example. At three years of age, Didi's parents prompted him to report a fight he had with a classmate at school. Didi's account cast himself as the victor. However, his older sister's narration of the same event portrayed Didi in a much less flattering light ("He lied. I saw with my own eyes that he was beaten and began to cry"). Didi's corpus of stories exemplifies another related feature of everyday stories, namely, that they can form thematically related clusters whose meanings inform one another. Over the course of the study (from 2,6 to 4,0), Didi and his family told 10 fight stories involving Didi as protagonist. In these stories, Didi and his conarrators strived to comprehend the appropriateness of his behavior in different contexts. While fighting with his sister at home was invariably considered a misdeed, fighting with classmates at school was sometimes viewed as appropriate or even courageous (e.g., standing up for himself). Also, over time, Didi seemed to develop more mature strategies for handling conflict; one fight story at 4,0 ended with him imagining what he would do in the future, "I could report to the teacher."

Repetitions of particular stories convey several metamessages that lay the groundwork for the personal narrative. Perhaps most fundamentally, they demonstrate to children that narrative can be used over and over again to revisit events in their lives and that those events can be looked at from different angles. Repetitions and thematically related stories highlight certain events, against each child's baseline of recurring stories, directing attention to particular concerns or problems to be pondered and informing children about their personal qualities and distinguishing characteristics. This underscores Cohler's point that narrative sense making is cultural and personal at the same time. Although the Chicago and Taipei children were constrained by different culturally salient interpretive biases, each child, working with those biases in the context of his or her own idiosyncratic experience, could not help but make meanings that were nuanced differently. By participating in repeated and related stories, children may come to see themselves as having a certain personality or occupying a certain position within the family (the one who is emotionally intense, the one who likes to fight). Over time, they may incorporate some of these stories into their personal narrative, construing them as lasting touchstones of self-defining meaning.

The dynamics of narrative in time are even more complex than this, however. Sometimes young children retell stories as a way of resolving emotional conflicts or gaining relief from distressing experiences. In such cases, the set of retellings has its own trajectory: an initially scary experience is coped with and ameliorated across successive retellings. In the final retelling, the child might announce, "Then I wasn't scared no more" (Miller, 1994). One interesting feature of this phenomenon is that once the conflict is resolved or the emotion alleviated, the story seems to lose its appeal, disappearing from the child's narrative horizon.

## Future Directions

In the conclusion to his essay, Cohler (1982) discusses the inadequacy of traditional psychological methods for the study of lives and argues that a new interpretive approach is needed. He says, "This interpretive approach to the study of the person parallels the approach actually used by persons in the successive interpretations or reconstruction of their own history as a personal narrative across the course of life" (p. 229). The take-home message of our chapter is that this process of successive interpretation is vigorously underway much earlier in life than Cohler realized and that there is a surprising degree of continuity between early meaning making and the personal narrative. This leads us to conclude that however momentous adolescence may be in the development of the personal narrative, important developments are happening during the interval between early childhood and adolescence. Here is a large and rich vein for future inquiry. For example, study of children's expanding temporal horizons in their stories of personal experience, including their use of temporal comparisons, age markers, and diverse time frames (e.g., future, hypothetical, habitual), would help to fill the gap in our understanding of how the personal narrative evolves developmentally (see Chafel, 1990; Preece, 1987; Sperry & Sperry, 1996).

There is, perhaps, a methodological reason why the developmental roots of the personal narrative have not received more attention. If the personal narrative cannot be understood without privileging the individual's own subjective accounts of their lives over the long term, and if children are too immature to provide such accounts, then there is no way to study the phenomenon in question. We hope that this chapter, based on ethnographic studies of stories as they arise in everyday life, convinces readers that this assumption is misguided. However, the more far-reaching point is that a great deal could be learned about the personal narrative, at any age, by adding unconventional methods to the mix (see, e.g., Lieblich's [Chapter 6 of this volume] fruitful use of participant observation and field journals). Ethnographic methods reckon with contingency, surprise, and serendipity. If narrative interpretation is a "wild card," to use Schiff's (Chapter 1 of this volume) felicitous term, these tools belong in the toolbox. We suspect, for example, that narrative reconstruction could be illuminated in new ways by asking adolescents to tell their personal narratives and reflect on how they came to imagine their lives in this way *and* by concurrently studying, via participant observation, their everyday narrative activity with friends and family.

When the ethnographic piece is part of the picture, one cannot help but be impressed by the sheer number and variety of narratives that impinge on people's lives across the life course (Hudley, Haight, & Miller, 2009) and by the complex forms of intertextuality that individuals weave (Miller et al., 2000). It is impossible to predict which of these stories will leave a mark. In *The Luminous Books of Childhood*, Maria Tatar (2009) discusses the testimony of distinguished writers who recall the passion, excitement, and unparalleled intensity of childhood encounters with particular written stories. Constructing the personal narrative involves more than revisiting and revising key events; it also involves selecting and culling stories and weighing alternative accounts. Without knowing how many and what kinds of stories are in the mix, how often some stories are replayed, and which stories are irresistible or unfriendly, it is hard to fully appreciate what a feat it is to make and remake the personal narrative.

NEW DIRECTIONS FOR CHILD AND ADOLESCENT DEVELOPMENT • DOI: 10.1002/cad

## References

Bamberg, M. G. W. (Ed.). (1997). Oral versions of personal experience: Three decades of narrative analysis [Special Issue]. *Journal of Narrative and Life History*, 7(1–4).

Bourdieu, P. (1990). *The logic of practice*. Stanford, CA: Stanford University Press.

Bruner, J. S. (1990). *Acts of meaning*. Cambridge, MA: Harvard University Press.

Chafel, J. A. (1990). "I'm doing much better than I did before": Are young children capable of verbalizing temporal comparisons of the self? *Early Child Development and Care*, 6, 271–286.

Chang, C.-J. (2004). Telling stories of experiences: Narrative development of young Chinese children. *Applied Psycholinguistics*, 25, 83–104.

Cohler, B. J. (1982). Personal narrative and life course. In P. Baltes & O. G. Brim (Eds.), *Life span development and behavior* (Vol. 4, pp. 205–241). New York, NY: Academic Press.

Cruikshank, J. (1990). *Life lived like a story: Life stories of three Yukon native elders*. Lincoln: University of Nebraska Press.

Engel, S. (1995). *The stories children tell: Making sense of the narrative of childhood*. New York, NY: W. H. Freeman.

Holland, D., Lachicotte, W., Skinner, D., & Cain, C. (1998). *Identity and agency in cultural worlds*. Cambridge, MA: Harvard University Press.

Hudley, E. P., Haight, W. L., & Miller, P. J. (2009). *"Raise up a child": Human development in an African-American family* (2nd ed.). Chicago, IL: Lyceum Press.

Labov, W., & Waletzky, J. (1967). Narrative analysis. In J. Helm (Ed.), *Essays on the verbal and visual arts* (pp. 12–44). Seattle: University of Washington Press.

Linde, C. (1989). *Life stories: The creation of coherence*. New York, NY: Oxford University Press.

Miller, P. J. (1994). Narrative practices: Their role in socialization and self-construction. In U. Neisser & R. Fivush (Eds.), *The remembering self: Construction and accuracy in the self-narrative* (pp. 158–179). New York, NY: Cambridge University Press.

Miller, P. J., Cho, G. E., & Bracey, J. (2005). Working-class children's experience through the prism of personal storytelling. *Human Development*, 48, 115–135.

Miller, P. J., Fung, H., Lin, S., Chen, C.-H., & Boldt, B. B. (2012). How socialization happens on the ground: Narrative practices as alternate socializing pathways in Taiwanese and European-American families. *Monographs of the Society for Research in Child Development* (Vol. 77, issue 1, Serial No. 302). Boston, MA: Wiley-Blackwell.

Miller, P. J., Fung, H., & Mintz, J. (1996). Self-construction through narrative practices: A Chinese and American comparison of early socialization. *Ethos*, 24, 1–44.

Miller, P. J., Hengst, J., Alexander, K. A., & Sperry, L. L. (2000). Narrative genres: Tools for creating alternate realities. In K. Rosengren, C. Johnson, & P. Harris (Eds.), *Imagining the impossible: The development of magical, scientific, and religious thinking in contemporary society* (pp. 212–246). New York, NY: Cambridge University Press.

Miller, P. J., Koven, M., & Lin, S. (2011). Narrative. In A. Duranti, E. Ochs, & B. B. Schieffelin (Eds.), *Handbook of language socialization* (pp. 190–208). Hoboken, NJ: Wiley-Blackwell.

Miller, P. J., & Moore, B. B. (1989). Narrative conjunctions of caregiver and child: A comparative perspective on socialization through stories. *Ethos*, 17, 43–64.

Miller, P. J., & Sperry, D. E. (2012). Déjà vu: The continuing misrecognition of low-income children's verbal abilities. In S. Fiske & H. Markus (Eds.), *Facing social class: How societal rank influences interaction* (pp. 109–130). New York, NY: Russell Sage.

Miller, P. J., & Sperry, L. L. (1988). Early talk about the past: The origins of conversational stories of personal experience. *Journal of Child Language*, 15, 293–315.

Nelson, K. (Ed.). (1989). *Narratives from the crib*. Cambridge, MA: Harvard University Press.

Nelson, K. (1996). *Language in cognitive development: The emergence of the mediated mind*. New York, NY: Cambridge University Press.

Ochs, E., & Capps, L. (2001). *Living narrative: Creating lives in everyday storytelling*. Cambridge, MA: Harvard University Press.

Pathman, T., Doydum, A., & Bauer, P. J. (2013). Bringing order to life events: Memory for the temporal order of autobiographical events over an extended period in school-aged children and adults. *Journal of Experimental Child Psychology, 115*, 309–325.

Peterson, C., Wang, Q., & Hou, Y. (2009). "When I was little": Childhood recollections in Chinese and European Canadian grade school children. *Child Development, 80*(2), 506–518.

Preece, A. (1987). The range of narrative forms conversationally produced by young children. *Journal of Child Language, 14*, 353–373.

Scribner, S., & Cole, M. (1981). *The psychology of literacy*. Cambridge, MA: Cambridge University Press.

Sperry, L. L., & Sperry, D. E. (1996). Early development of narrative skills. *Cognitive Development, 11*, 443–465.

Tatar, M. (2009). The luminous books of childhood. In R. A. Shweder, T. Bidell, A. Dailey, S. Dixon, P. J. Miller, & J. Modell (Eds.), *The child: An encyclopedic companion* (p. 575). Chicago, IL: University of Chicago Press.

Wang, Q., Peterson, C., & Hou, Y. (2010). Children dating childhood memories. *Memory, 18*, 754–762.

Wertsch, J. V. (1991). *Voices of the mind: A sociocultural approach to mediated action*. Cambridge, MA: Harvard University Press.

Wilson, A., Hoshino-Browne, E., & Ross, M. (2002). Spontaneous temporal and social comparisons in children's conflict narratives. In I. Walker & H. J. Smith (Eds.), *Relative deprivation: Specification, development and integration* (pp. 313–331). Cambridge, UK: Cambridge University Press.

## Notes

1. Labov and Waletzky's (1967) sample consisted of European-American and African-American individuals who had not finished high school. They lived in a variety of rural and urban areas including Harlem, the Lower East Side of New York City, and Martha's Vineyard.

2. We examined 470 stories of young children's past experiences from Chinese families in Taipei and 420 stories from European-American families in Chicago, encompassing the period from 2,6 to 4,0 years. In both cases, roughly 0.06 of the stories involved a temporal comparison, that is, the child protagonist's current (or future) self was compared to an earlier self. See Miller et al. (2012) for a description of the two samples and of the procedures for recording, transcribing, and analyzing stories.

3. In a study based on parents' reports of children's conflict narratives, Wilson, Hoshino-Browne, and Ross (2002) found that temporal comparisons were extremely rare in 3- to 5-year-olds. However, in a review article, Chafel (1990) concluded that young children are able to express temporal comparisons about the self from three years onward, called for more study concerning the role that temporal comparisons play in the development of young children's self-understanding.

PEGGY J. MILLER *is a professor emerita in the Department of Psychology and Department of Communication at the University of Illinois at Urbana-Champaign.*

EVA CHIAN-HUI CHEN *is an assistant professor in the Department of Psychological Sciences at the Benedictine College.*

MEGAN OLIVAREZ *is the research coordinator of the Childrearing Lab in the Department of Psychology at the University of Illinois at Urbana-Champaign.*

NEW DIRECTIONS FOR CHILD AND ADOLESCENT DEVELOPMENT • DOI: 10.1002/cad

Habermas, T., & Hatiboğlu, N. (2014). Contextualizing the self: The emergence of a bio-graphical understanding in adolescence. In B. Schiff (Ed.), *Rereading Personal Narrative and Life Course. New Directions for Child and Adolescent Development, 145*, 29–41.

3

# Contextualizing the Self: The Emergence of a Biographical Understanding in Adolescence

*Tilmann Habermas, Neşe Hatiboğlu*

## Abstract

*In adolescence, remembering the personal past and understanding what kind of person one is intertwine to form a story of one's life as the most extant, in-formative, and flexible form of self-representation. In adolescence, the striving for self-coherence translates into a quest for global coherence of the life story. We suggest that contextualizing is a fifth means for creating global coherence in life narratives besides the cultural concept of biography, temporal, causal-motivational, and thematic coherence. We present three kinds of contextualizing in life narratives, the temporal macrostructure, sociohistorical contextualizing of one's life, and hierarchical and linear segmenting of the text and life. These three forms of contextualizing in life narratives by their authors are comple-mented by three forms of contextual influences on life narratives analyzed by researchers, namely the historical, personal, and communicative situation in which they are recounted. Contextualizing is exemplified by the life narrative of a young migrant.* © 2014 Wiley Periodicals, Inc.

New Directions for Child and Adolescent Development, no. 145, Fall 2014 © 2014 Wiley Periodicals, Inc.
Published online in Wiley Online Library (wileyonlinelibrary.com). • DOI: 10.1002/cad.20065

B ert Cohler achieved a unique identity as a psychologist and psycho-analyst with an understanding of his disciplines as basically inter-pretative sciences which can learn from neighboring fields in the humanities. He was deeply influenced by his early experience in the psycho-analytic Orthogenic School in Chicago as well as by the broad inter-disciplinary programs of the Committee on Human Development at the University of Chicago and Social Relations at Harvard. These institutional and intellectual contexts offered Cohler horizons of which he made unique use to become his own brand of "life course social scientist" (Cohler & Galatzer-Levy, 2000) who took a genuinely interpretative approach to indi-vidual lives.

Bert Cohler's (1982) masterpiece *Personal Narrative and Life Course* in-spired one of us (Tilmann Habermas) to turn to the life story not only as an object of clinical dialogue and description, but also, in the form of nar-rative, as an object of systematic psychological research. Cohler effortlessly weaves social theory, history, psychology, and psychoanalysis into an inte-grated argument, or, better, a vision of an entire research program.

Cohler pointed out adolescence as the developmental phase in which sociocognitive development opens the possibility to access cultural forms such as the diary (Bernfeld, 1931), to autobiographical self-presentation, and, more generally, to the format of the life story and biographical thinking. Although Erikson (1968), inspired by his teacher Bernfeld, elaborated the life story as an instrument for psychoanalytic understanding and as the most mature form of psychosocial identity that developed in adolescence, only Cohler (1982) actually linked the attainment of an integrated subjective identity, a feeling of coherence and self-continuity, to adolescent cognitive maturation that allows an understanding of personal and collective history (p. 220).

Here, we pick up two concerns of Cohler's paper and elaborate their significance for the life story and its development in adolescence: coher-ence and context. We first discuss the development of life story *coherence* in adolescence; then we suggest *contextualizing* as a fifth device for creating coherence. We illustrate the characteristics of a well-developed, coherent life narrative in young adulthood with extracts from a life narrative by a young woman with a migrant background.

## Coherent Life Narratives Develop Only in Adolescence

Cohler (1982) linked both the intelligibility of a life narrative and its func-tion to provide a subjective sense of self-continuity to the compatibility of the form of the life narrative with "socially shared expectations that stories should have a beginning, a middle, and an end, and in which the mean-ing of expected and eruptive life events is understood in terms of socially shared definitions of the significance and timing of these events" (p. 205). In previous research, we elaborated on Cohler's concept and attempted to

NEW DIRECTIONS FOR CHILD AND ADOLESCENT DEVELOPMENT • DOI: 10.1002/cad

define the formal properties of global text coherence of life narratives in terms of their temporal, causal-motivational, and thematic aspects (Habermas & Bluck, 2000). Global temporal coherence allows listeners to place events at specific times in life. Global causal-motivational coherence explains and motivates changes in life, showing how the narrator attempted to lead a life guided by values. Global thematic coherence is created by implicit themes and explicit comparisons between heterogeneous elements of life, pointing to underlying constancies across change. We measured these three aspects of global text coherence in life narratives in three different ways. To do justice to the global character of global coherence, we rated each of these three aspects on the entire life narrative. We defined three rating scales for how well the reader is temporally oriented in the narrator's life, for how well the life narrative transmits a sense of how the narrator has developed, and for how well the narrator succeeds to create implicit and possibly also explicit thematic coherence across heterogeneous events. To identify some of the specific verbal means that contribute to the three aspects of global coherence, we coded several sets of local indicators for each aspect, including temporal indicators and autobiographical arguments that link local events to distant parts of life (e.g., biographical antecedents or consequences) and to the development of personality (Habermas, 2011; Habermas & de Silveira, 2008). Finally, we measured the temporal macrostructure, which we will explain later.

Following Cohler's insistence that narrative coherence relies upon a shared social understanding of what is a good life narrative, we defined a fourth aspect of global coherence as the consistency of the life narrative with a shared cultural concept of biography. Specifically, we suggest that there is a shared skeleton of life narratives, consisting of a set of biographically salient life events and their normative timing (Habermas & Bluck, 2000). We measured knowledge of the cultural concept of biography by comparing judgments of biographical salience and age norms for selected life events with a norm established by a group of young adults (Habermas, 2007). Berntsen and Rubin (2004) termed this normative biographical skeleton a *life script*, stressing its normative and linear temporal nature.

In the past decade, several studies have substantiated Bert Cohler's claim that while the ability to narrate specific events or stories is acquired between early and mid-childhood, the acquisition of the life story format is a later achievement of adolescence (Bohn & Berntsen, 2008, 2013; Habermas & de Silveira, 2008; Habermas & Paha, 2001). This development has been confirmed longitudinally over an eight-year period (Köber, Schmiedek, & Habermas, 2014). Others have shown the emergence across adolescence of the use of autobiographical arguments also in other text types, namely in narratives of single critical life events (Chen, McAnally, Wang, & Reese, 2012; Grysman & Hudson, 2010). In single-event narratives, autobiographical arguments link the specific event to earlier or later events in life and to the narrator's personal development (Habermas, 2011), thereby integrating the event into the life story without narrating an entire life. We have thus identified verbal means which people use to construct continuity in their lives. However, Cohler's claim that a coherent life story is used for establishing and maintaining a subjective sense of self-continuity (cf. Habermas & Köber, in press; Prebble, Addis, & Tippett, 2013) remains to be tested.

## Contextualizing as a Fifth Aspect of Global Coherence of Life Narratives

Drawing on other texts is a fundamental mechanism of interpretation. In life narratives, persons draw upon earlier or present experiences to understand past actions. Narrative is a prime cultural tool for contextualizing and understanding human action. To understand an action, which by definition is motivated, it needs to be embedded in a story (e.g., von Wright, 1971). Context is a requirement of narrative, which is fulfilled by the orienting section. And, recontextualizing the results of actions in a final evaluation is also a normative property of narratives (e.g., Labov & Waletzky, 1967). This internal contextualizing of the plot is framed by an external contextualizing of the communicative situation, which is reflected in the narrative itself by its abstract and coda.

We present three internal contextualizing devices that enable narrators to reflect on the contexts of their actions and their lives (evaluative elaboration of beginnings and endings, social contextualization of life, and text segmenting). Consequently, we also present three contexts external to narratives that influence them (history and culture, the present situation in life, and the present communicative situation). We exemplify the role of contextualizing with a 15-minute life narrative told by 24-year-old Ebru, a Turkish-German young woman whose family migrated to Germany before she was born. This situation renders the cultural context more salient and forces individuals to choose more consciously cultural contexts and values to identify with.

## Internal Contexts in Life Narratives

In this section, we describe three devices, internal to life narratives, which allow persons to contextualize their stories.

**Narrative Beginnings, Middles, and Endings.** Following Aristotle's (1987) dictum that coherence in tragedy is created by embedding the plot in a structured beginning and ending, and Cohler's (1982) suggestion that the same may be true for life narratives, we analyzed how beginnings and endings of life narratives are structured to contribute to global coherence (Habermas, 2006). We judged the maturity of beginnings and endings by the degree of elaboration and by age differences. Mature beginnings started with birth, indicating date and place and, sometimes, a narrative about the circumstances of birth, foreshadowing later developments. Mature endings led to the present and involved both a retrospective evaluation and a resulting outlook onto expectations and plans for the future. Our ordinal scales for the maturity of beginnings and endings showed a cross-sectional (Bohn & Berntsen, 2008; Habermas, Ehlert-Lerche, & de Silveira, 2009) as well as a longitudinal increase between late childhood and young adulthood (Köber et al., 2014). Since beginnings and endings are defined temporally, we also defined the middle section as basically determined by a linear chronological sequence, deviations from which need to be explicated to keep the listener temporally oriented (cf. Genette, 1982). Temporal linearity increased strongly between late childhood and early adolescence (Habermas et al., 2009), but marked deviations from a linear order increased across adulthood (Köber et al., 2014), which we interpreted as a sign of life narratives being narrated more artfully later in life.

We termed this structure of beginning, middle, and ending the *temporal macrostructure* of life narratives. The quality of the components of the temporal macrostructure correlated most with temporal coherence compared to causal-motivational and thematic coherence, justifying our choice of name (Habermas et al., 2009).

The prominence of causal-motivational and thematic coherence is evident in the beginnings of Ebru's life narrative that starts with birth and the family context:

> I was born into a very crowded family. My mother, father, paternal uncles and aunts, we were all living together in one house. Being the first child in the family, being the first grandchild, I was a terribly spoiled child. I was born in Düsseldorf in 1986. I really was the very special child in the family. My paternal grandmother still tells me about my childhood. I was quite lucky to be born into a crowded, nice family.

The beginning is highly elaborated, setting the theme for later life. Ebru starts with birth, providing both year and place of birth.

**Social Contextualization of Life.** Another way to contextualize a life is to embed it in a family constellation, a family history, a socioeconomic and sociocultural situation, and a historical situation. The initial context cannot be directly remembered but is learned from others or is reconstructed. An individual's social and historical context may be used to define their identity (Strauss, 1959). Historical context, however, is mentioned in everyday life narratives only if historical events have strongly impacted the person's life, typically a war (Brown, Hansen, Lee, Vanderveen, & Conrad, 2012).

During adolescence, initial family constellation, social-economic context, and family history are mentioned increasingly in life narratives (Köber & Habermas, 2013). This increase is rendered possible by the adolescent's developing understanding of society and the contextual variables related to socioeconomic status (Barrett & Buchanan-Barrow, 2005; Furnham & Stacey, 1991). Only in adolescence does the understanding of economics

NEW DIRECTIONS FOR CHILD AND ADOLESCENT DEVELOPMENT • DOI: 10.1002/cad

begin to encompass the abstract levels of the economic system (Berti & Bombi, 1988) and of historical developments (cf. Barton, 2008). The growing appreciation of the role of the wider, nonimmediate social context is reflected in an increasing use of nonagentic linguistic constructions in life narratives across adolescence (de Silveira & Habermas, 2011).

Rereading Ebru's opening sentences, we see that there is no birth story in Ebru's narrative, but the social context of her birth is used as a formative experience. The listener understands that being the firstborn, and the first to be born on foreign soil, renders Ebru especially valuable to the entire extended family who has recently migrated. Consequently, the listener understands why she had been such a special child to so many people in her family.

> Then I started kindergarten. I didn't know German well because my family used to watch Turkish TV and only spoke Turkish. There were only a few Turkish people in the neighborhood. Now there are more, but there were only a few in those years. I was the only Turkish child in kindergarten, and since I didn't understand German well, I couldn't make any friends. I began to learn the language little by little only later when I went to school. [ ... ] The situation was more balanced in primary school. I made many Turkish friends and I had a number of German friends, too. I was also beginning to understand German. Accordingly, I started to get rid of my troubles there.

In this passage, Ebru explains the social and historical contexts of her upbringing and uses it to explain her very personal problems of social isolation.

> Then I enrolled in the Gymnasium in fifth grade [German grammar school; this still is exceptional for children of migrants]. I had great difficulties in the first years because I started to have problems with the language due to the higher linguistic requirements there. I failed seventh grade. My mom and everybody were angry at me. I mean, that was the worst part of it, because my paternal grandfather and uncles used to say: "Dear girl, you are the oldest child in our family, you know, you have a number of cousins and a sister to follow in your footsteps. Therefore you should choose a good path in life so that they can see you as a role model." I was under a lot of pressure. Back then I realized the significance of school to some extent. I started to understand what my mother, father, and grandfather were trying to tell me. I realized the importance of school, and I started to study really hard. [ ... ] I always wanted to study, and I knew that you could achieve something in life through education.

Ebru's narrative continues with migration-related language problems and educational difficulties. She uses the value of education in her family as a context to describe the personal meaning of failing and its consequences.

NEW DIRECTIONS FOR CHILD AND ADOLESCENT DEVELOPMENT • DOI: 10.1002/cad

The significance of her standing in the extended family recurs. We can assume that the general social and historical situation of the family determined the role of education for upward social mobility. Ebru narrates how a specific event, her family's reaction to her failing seventh grade, motivated her to identify with a family value, which in turn is explained by the social context. Explaining a central value by what one learned from a specific experience is an autobiographical argument that links temporal information with an enduring defining feature of personality.

**Text Segmentation.** Life narratives are segmented so that larger segments provide contexts for more focal parts (Ji, 2008; Passonneau & Litman, 1997). Segments can be specified in terms of text types and in terms of temporal extension and inclusion. Life narratives contain three types of texts: single-event narratives, chronicles, and arguments (Linde, 1993). Single-event narratives may contain contextualizing information about the particular event reported. Chronicles and arguments provide the larger context to specific episodes. In order to establish continuity, single stories are connected by chronicles that summarize the major events of a given period and thereby provide context for stories and link them. Dorthe Thomsen (2009) calls chronicles *life story chapters*. Arguments are atemporal and allow narrators to take a distanced, third person, perspective on their lives (Linde, 1987; Rosenthal, 1993). Arguments may explicitly link single events with each other and with the global structure of the life narrative by announcing, summarizing, evaluating, or explaining (Schütze, 1984).

Personal memories have a nested structure (Neisser, 1986), with more specific events embedded in extended events, which in turn are embedded in life phases (Conway, Singer, & Tagini, 2004). Life narratives are also segmented thematically and temporally by nesting less inclusive in more inclusive segments (Rosenthal, 1995; Schütze, 1984). Segment borders are signaled by paralinguistic devices such as changes in pitch (e.g., Ozcan, 2012). However, specific episodes are not necessarily bracketed by chronicles. Rather, episodes with a turning point are often used to demarcate transitions between life phases (Rosenthal, 1995; Strauss, 1959; cf. Thomsen, Pillemer, & Ivcevic, 2011). In two large-scale studies of life narratives, half of the turning point episodes coincided with conventional, normative life transitions (Clausen, 1995; Lehr, 1976). Repeated events serve to describe what was typical for an extended period of time (Habermas & Diel, 2013).

The use of segments to narrate extended periods of time and the use of arguments increase steeply across adolescence. Thus, specific events are more and more selected over this period not just because they are in themselves memorable, but because they can exemplify or explain (Chen, McAnally, & Reese, 2013; Habermas, Diel, & Welzer, 2013).

Ebru provides a good example of the use of a turning point event to describe a global aspect of her life narrative.

[ ... ] Later on, I lost two of my closest friends. They were two Turkish girls with whom I used to play football. It was a traffic accident. [ ... ] One day, on our way to football practice, they were run over by a car and killed. This is the worst thing that ever happened to me. I asked myself about the meaning of life. I thought things like 'Such an event happens out of the blue,' 'will I die too?,' 'I could have been there too.' Then, as I passed through my adolescent years, I found religion, I found myself in God. I started to perform the prayer; I started to fast. [ ... ] Religion is very important for me. The most important thing in life is religion for me.

Ebru uses a turning point event to segment her life. She explains how she found religion and a worldview, which implicitly ties her identity, rooted in a very personal experience, to the culture of her parents and family.

## External Contexts of Life Narratives

Contextualizing is thus a device for creating global coherence in life narratives. At the same time, life narratives are always situated in, influenced by, and geared toward multiple contexts.

**Historical Context.** As demonstrated by Erikson in his case studies (e.g., Erikson, 1958) and more systematically by Elder (1974/1999), historical, cultural, and social contexts strongly influence the actual course a life takes. The influence of historical circumstances can be studied by comparing cohorts, or by studying the impact of sudden political changes on the life course, such as Barbara and Winfried Junge's long-term film portrait of the students in two East German school classes between 1961 and 2007. In addition, the actual form of narration is conditioned by the historical, cultural, and social contexts. This is shown in the history of the literary genre of autobiography, which is a relatively recent development of the 18th century (Holdenried, 2000). Cohler (2007) provided a highly illustrative study of how the form of life stories changes historically by comparing 10 published autobiographies by gay men, two of whom were born in each decade between the 1930s and 1970s. He demonstrated not only how gay emancipation and the HIV epidemic shaped the lives of gay men, but also the way they narrated their lives by following, for example, a cultural master narrative of the coming out experience that emerged in the 1970s (cf. Hammack & Toolis, Chapter 4 of this volume).

Providing yet another example of how cultural narratives shape individual life narratives, Cohler (2008) contrasted autobiographical accounts of Shoah survivors written in the immediate aftermath of the war and over half a century later. The earlier personal accounts reflect the absence of a public narrative about the Shoah, while the later narrative reflected the influence of a specific public model of redemption narrative. Comparing diaries written by two adolescents living in Poland during the Shoah, Cohler (2012) showed how the ability for autobiographical reasoning emerged in adolescence and was used to cope with deteriorating chances for surviving the German program to kill all Jews.

Back to Ebru, her family's migration story plays a crucial role in her life narrative. The German attitude and policy toward immigrants significantly shaped the second generation's life course.

**Personal Context.** The narrator's present situation in life defines their perspective on their personal past, shifting as life is lived and as concerns, values, and identities change in response to both normative developmental milestones and transformations triggered by nonnormative events (Cohler, 1982). Josselson (2000) demonstrated how the childhood memory of a wedding changed over three reminiscing occasions across a total of 22 years, depending on the rememberer's maturation and how the meaning of the memory of a first love relationship changed over 35 years (Josselson, 2009). Schiff (2005) compared an Auschwitz survivor's memories at 38 and 51 years after the Shoah. While the memory itself remained fairly stable, its interpretation and evaluation changed, depending both on changes in how the dominant culture dealt with Auschwitz memories and on personal changes in the narrator. Massie and Szajnberg (2005) interviewed 76 individuals at age 30 whose development had been well documented during their first five years and who had been interviewed at age 18 by different researchers. They compared the participants' memories at 30 with the earlier observations, again showing how childhood memories are selected and formed by present concerns. In addition, they noted how childhood memories at age 30 seemed to be much more accessible and extensively narrated than at age 18, when the present had been more predominant.

At the time of the telling of her life, Ebru was looking forward to finishing her studies and beginning to work. She reconstructed her life in such a way that two dominant motives, rooted in important life experiences, lead straight to an imminent future. She merges education and religion to explain her choice of career and her perspective on her future work as a psychologist:

> [ . . . ] I was dying to become a psychologist because I saw it as an occupation which paralleled religious principles, helping people, passing on my knowledge to others. Therefore it was the occupation closest to my thoughts. Now I am very happy about the internship, and I think this occupation has the potential to satisfy you a lot. Thank God, I have achieved my goal, I am very happy about it.

The narrative ends in the present with Ebru finishing her university studies in psychology. She, thereby, creates coherence between present concerns, past experiences, and future aspirations as well as with her enduring worldview. This is the most elaborate form of ending, which both evaluates the past and bases her outlook on the personal future on life experiences.

Additionally, looking at the entire narrative, we see that the narrative follows a chronological order and displays a mature temporal macrostructure.

**Communicative Context.** Finally, the specific situation in which personal memories or a life story is told influences the selection and evaluation of narrated events. Narrators tune their narratives to the listener's knowledge, values, and interests. The relationship to the listener motivates more or less self-exposure, and the communicative aims guide the way narrators present themselves in life narratives (Cohler, 1982; Pasupathi, 2001).

Ebru knows that she is talking to a Turkish psychologist and she is talking to her in Turkish. This possibly motivated her to stress the cultural and the professional issues more than she might have if she had told her life to a German who is not a psychologist. In that case she would have had to explain more about Turkish culture.

## Conclusion

We chose a young adult's life narrative to exemplify the role of narrative in adolescence because in retrospect developmental processes can be better explicated. Ebru's life narrative exemplifies how adolescents learn to shape their identity by rooting commitments in highly personal experiences via autobiographical reasoning, in failing seventh grade and in the death of two friends. To objectify the self by acknowledging the role of social context is a highly mature form of autobiographical reasoning that helps in personally choosing values and establishing ego identity. The resulting values, education and religion, might as well have resulted from an automatic unquestioned carryover of infantile identifications with parental values, that is, a foreclosed identity. But the life narrative clarifies that they have been adopted in an active exploration of the meaning of personal experiences. Had we granted more than 15 minutes to Ebru to recount her life, she might have clarified further whether her turn to religion was also a way of identifying with her parents' cultural heritage. Ebru's narrative appears to indicate that her religiousness is not traditional, that is, adopted without any exploration and reflection, but self-chosen.

Thus, adolescence is the phase in life in which the earlier development of language acquisition and of narrative competence (Miller, Chen, & Olivarez, Chapter 2 of this volume) is further elaborated into the highly specific ability to construct a story about the individual's personal development across life. The life story requires integrating memories and self-concept into a coherent overall account. Adolescence thus brings a new biographical quality to individuals' speaking and thinking about others and themselves. This ability allows adolescents to recognize the influence of their own familial, sociocultural, and historical contexts. At the same time, the ability for constructing the life story in itself appears to be a historically specific requirement, which involves culturally specific shared biographical norms and concepts. The basic ability develops across adolescence and provides individuals in adulthood and old age with a tool to give direction to their lives as well as to accommodate to the chances and hazards of life.

Thus, we suggest to qualify Schiff's (Chapter 1 of this volume) first thesis (the self is a narrative project) in light of his second thesis (each developmental phase has its own narrative characteristic), underlining Cohler's observation that only in adolescence does the self acquire a consistently narrative quality. This adds to the normative requirement of personal consistency and coherence a temporal, biographical dimension, and adds to narrative textual coherence and the means to achieve personal coherence (Habermas & Köber, in press).

## References

Aristotle. (1987). *Poetics*. Chapel Hill: University of North Carolina.

Barrett, M., & Buchanan-Barrow, E. (Eds.). (2005). *Children's understanding of society*. London, UK: Taylor & Francis.

Barton, K. C. (2008). Research on students' ideas about history. In L. S. Levstik & C. A. Tyson (Eds.), *Handbook of research in social studies education* (pp. 239–258). New York, NY: Routledge.

Bernfeld, S. (1931). *Trieb und Tradition im Jugendalter*. Leipzig: Barth.

Berntsen, D., & Rubin, D. C. (2004). Cultural life scripts structure recall from autobiographical memory. *Memory & Cognition, 32,* 427–442.

Berti, A. E., & Bombi, A. S. (1988). *The child's construction of economics*. Cambridge, UK: Cambridge University Press.

Bohn, A., & Berntsen, D. (2008). Life story development in childhood: The development of life story abilities and the acquisition of cultural life scripts from late middle childhood to adolescence. *Developmental Psychology, 44,* 1135–1147.

Bohn, A., & Berntsen, D. (2013). The future is bright and predictable: The development of prospective life stories across childhood and adolescence. *Developmental Psychology, 49,* 1232–1241.

Brown, N. R., Hansen, T. G., Lee, P., Vanderveen, S. A., & Conrad, F. G. (2012). Historically defined autobiographical periods: Their origins and implications. In D. Berntsen & D. C. Rubin (Eds.), *Understanding autobiographical memory: Theories and approaches* (pp. 160–180). Cambridge, UK: Cambridge University Press.

Chen, Y., McAnally, H. M., & Reese, E. (2013). Development in the organization of episodic memories in middle childhood and adolescence. *Frontiers in Behavioral Neuroscience, 7,* 1–9.

Chen, Y., McAnally, H. M., Wang, Q., & Reese, E. (2012). The coherence of critical event narratives and adolescents' psychological functioning. *Memory, 20,* 667–681.

Clausen, J. (1995). *American lives*. Berkeley: University of California Press.

Cohler, B. J. (1982). Personal narrative and life course. *Lifespan Development and Behavior, 4,* 205–241.

Cohler, B. J. (2007). *Writing desire: Sixty years of gay autobiography*. Madison: University of Wisconsin Press.

Cohler, B. J. (2008). Two lives, two times. Life writing after Shoah. *Narrative Inquiry, 18,* 1–28.

Cohler, B. J. (2012). Confronting destruction: Social context and life story in the diaries of two adolescents in Eastern European ghettos during the Shoa. *American Journal of Orthopsychiatry, 82,* 220–230.

Cohler, B. J., & Galatzer-Levy, R. M. (2000). *The course of gay and lesbian lives*. Chicago, IL: University of Chicago Press.

Conway, M. A., Singer, J. A., & Tagini, A. (2004). The self in autobiographical memory: Correspondence and coherence. *Social Cognition, 22,* 491–529.

de Silveira, C., & Habermas, T. (2011). Narrative means to manage responsibility in life narratives across adolescence. *Journal of Genetic Psychology, 172,* 1–20.

Elder, G. H., Jr. (1974/1999). *Children of the great depression: Social change in life experience* (25th anniversary ed.). Boulder, CO: Westview Press.

Erikson, E. H. (1958). *Young man Luther.* New York, NY: Norton.

Erikson, E. H. (1968). *Identity: Youth and crisis.* New York, NY: Norton.

Furnham, A., & Stacey, B. (1991). *Young people's understanding of society.* London, UK: Routledge.

Genette, G. (1982). *Narrative discourse.* Ithaca, NY: Cornell University Press.

Grysman, A., & Hudson, J. A. (2010). Abstracting and extracting: Causal coherence and the development of the life story. *Memory, 18,* 565–580.

Habermas, T. (2006). Kann ich auch ganz, ganz am Anfang anfangen? Wie Jugendliche lernen, Lebenserzählungen zu eröffnen und beenden. In H. Welzer & H. J. Markowitsch (Eds.), *Warum Menschen sich erinnern: Fortschritte der interdisziplinären Gedächtnisforschung* (pp. 256–275). Stuttgart, GE: Klett-Cotta.

Habermas, T. (2007). How to tell a life: The development of the cultural concept of biography across the lifespan. *Journal of Cognition and Development, 8,* 1–31.

Habermas, T. (2011). Autobiographical reasoning: Arguing and narrating from a biographical perspective. In T. Habermas (Ed.), *New Directions for Child and Adolescent Development: No. 131. The development of autobiographical reasoning in adolescence and beyond* (pp. 1–17). San Francisco, CA: Jossey-Bass.

Habermas, T., & Bluck, S. (2000). Getting a life: The development of the life story in adolescence. *Psychological Bulletin, 126,* 748–769.

Habermas, T., & de Silveira, C. (2008). The development of global coherence in life narratives across adolescence: Temporal, causal, and thematic aspects. *Developmental Psychology, 44,* 707–721.

Habermas, T., & Diel, V. (2013). The episodicity of verbal reports of personally significant autobiographical memories: Vividness correlates with narrative text quality more than with detailedness or memory specificity. *Frontiers in Behavioral Neuroscience, 7,* 1–13.

Habermas, T., Diel, V., & Welzer, H. (2013). Lifespan trends of autobiographical remembering. *Consciousness & Cognition, 22,* 1061–1072.

Habermas, T., Ehlert-Lerche, S., & de Silveira, C. (2009). The development of the temporal macrostructure of life narratives across adolescence. *Journal of Personality, 77,* 527–560.

Habermas, T., & Köber, C. (in press). Autobiographical reasoning is constitutive for narrative identity: The role of the life story for personal continuity. In K. C. McLean & M. Syed (Eds.), *The Oxford handbook of identity development.* Oxford, UK: Oxford University Press.

Habermas, T., & Paha, C. (2001). The development of coherence in adolescents' life narratives. *Narrative Inquiry, 11,* 35–54.

Holdenried, M. (2000). *Autobiographie.* Stuttgart, GE: Reclam.

Ji, S. (2008). What do paragraph divisions indicate in narrative texts? *Journal of Pragmatics, 40,* 1719–1730.

Josselson, R. (2000). Stability and change in early memories over 22 years: Themes, variations, and cadenzas. *Bulletin of the Menninger Clinic, 64,* 462–481.

Josselson, R. (2009). The present of the past: Dialogues with memory over time. *Journal of Personality, 77,* 1–22.

Köber, C., & Habermas, T. (2013, June). *Contextualizing one's life in the micro- and macrosystem of society in narrated life stories.* Poster session presented at the conference Social Perspectives on Autobiographical Memory, Arhus, Denmark.

Köber, C., Schmiedek, F., & Habermas, T. (2014). *Characterizing lifespan development of three aspects of coherence in life narratives: A cohort-sequential study.* Manuscript submitted for publication.

Labov, W., & Waletzky, J. (1967). Narrative analysis: Oral versions of personal experience. In I. Helm (Ed.), *Essays on the verbal and visual arts. Proceedings of the 1966 Annual Spring Meeting of the American Ethnological Society* (pp. 12–44). Seattle: University of Washington Press.

Lehr, U. (1976). Zur Frage der Gliederung des menschlichen Lebenslaufs [On the structure of the human life course]. *Aktuelle Gerontologie, 6,* 337–345.

Linde, C. (1987). Explanatory systems in oral life stories. In D. Holland & N. Quinn (Eds.), *Cultural models in language and thought* (pp. 343–366). Cambridge, UK: Cambridge University Press.

Linde, C. (1993). *Life stories.* New York, NY: Cambridge University Press.

Massie, H. N., & Szajnberg, N. M. (2005). *Lives across time: Pathways to emotional health and emotional illness from birth to 30.* New York, NY: Xlibris.

Neisser, U. (1986). Nested structure in autobiographical memory. In D. C. Rubin (Ed.), *Autobiographical memory* (pp. 71–81). New York, NY: Cambridge University Press.

Ozcan, M. (2012). Suprasegmentals in the definition of narrative and intonational patterns in Turkish oral narratives. *Text & Talk, 32,* 797–819.

Passonneau, R. J., & Litman, D. J. (1997). Discourse segmentation by human and automated means. *Computational Linguistics, 23,* 103–139.

Pasupathi, M. (2001). The social construction of the personal past and its implications for adult development. *Psychological Bulletin, 127,* 651–672.

Prebble, S. C., Addis, D. R., & Tippett, L. J. (2013). Autobiographical memory and sense of self. *Psychological Bulletin, 139,* 815–840.

Rosenthal, G. (1993). Reconstruction of life stories. In R. Josselson & A. Liebich (Eds.), *The narrative study of lives* (Vol. 1, pp. 59–91). Newbury Park, CA: Sage.

Rosenthal, G. (1995). *Erlebte und erzählte Lebensgeschichte* [The lived and narrated life story]. Frankfurt, GE: Campus.

Schiff, B. (2005). Telling in time: Interpreting consistency and change in the life stories of Holocaust survivors. *International Journal of Aging and Human Development, 60,* 189–212.

Schütze, F. (1984). Kognitive Figuren des autobiographischen Stegreiferzählens [Cognitive structures of improvised personal narratives]. In M. Kohli & G. Robert (Eds.), *Biographie und soziale Wirklichkeit* (pp. 78–118). Stuttgart, GE: Metzler.

Strauss, A. (1959). *Mirror and masks: The search for identity.* New York, NY: Free Press.

Thomsen, D. K. (2009). There is more to life stories than memories. *Memory, 17,* 445–457.

Thomsen, D. K., Pillemer, D. P., & Ivcevic, Z. (2011). Life story chapters, specific memories, and the reminiscence bump. *Memory, 19,* 167–279.

von Wright, G. H. (1971). *Explanation and understanding.* Ithaca, NY: Cornell University Press.

TILMANN HABERMAS *is a professor of psychoanalysis at the Department of Psychology, Goethe University Frankfurt.*

NEŞE HATIBOĞLU *is a PhD candidate at the Department of Psychology, Goethe University Frankfurt.*

Hammack, P. L., & Toolis, E. (2014). Narrative and the social construction of adulthood. In B. Schiff (Ed.), *Rereading Personal Narrative and Life Course. New Directions in Child and Adolescent Development, 145*, 43–56.

4

# Narrative and the Social Construction of Adulthood

*Phillip L. Hammack, Erin Toolis*

## Abstract

*This chapter develops three points of elaboration and theoretical expansion upon Cohler's (1982) treatise on personal narrative and life course. First, we highlight Cohler's emphasis on an interpretive, idiographic approach to the study of lives and reveal the radicalism of this approach, particularly in its ability to interrogate the lived experience of social categorization. Second, we link Cohler's position directly to cultural-historical activity theory (CHAT) and consider the link between inner and social speech through the idea of narrative engagement. Finally, following Cohler's life course perspective on human development, we suggest that adulthood is best conceived as a cultural discourse to which individuals orient their personal narratives through a dynamic process of narrative engagement rather than a clearly demarcated life stage. Emerging adulthood is linked to cultural and economic processes of globalization in the 21st century and challenges static notions of social roles traditionally associated with compulsory heterosexuality (e.g., marriage and parenthood). Narrative processes in emerging adulthood occur through both situated storytelling and the formation of a life story that provides coherence and social meaning, both of which have key implications for social stasis and change. © 2014 Wiley Periodicals, Inc.*

...There are no events or facts regarding lives which are independent of interpretations which are made of them—just as, in studying history more generally, concern is with the adequacy of the narrative or interpretation, rather
than with the actuality of the events.

Cohler (1982, p. 228)

Martin Duberman, the scholar and pioneer of early gay and lesbian studies, was born in 1930 and experienced early adulthood
in the 1950s and early 1960s—a time in which the gay and lesbian civil rights movement was emerging but before the Stonewall riots that
brought national visibility (Duberman, 1993). He experienced adulthood
and developed an understanding of his sexual identity at a time in which
homosexuality remained a diagnosable mental illness. Describing his early
adulthood, Duberman (1991) said, "We accepted as given that we as homo-
sexuals could never reach 'full adult maturity'...: marrying, settling down,
having a family" (p. 344). Like many gay men of his generation, Duberman
struggled in early adulthood to construct a personal narrative consistent
with dominant cultural expectations for the life course.

Today's young adults with same-sex desire, in contrast to those of
Duberman's generation, inhabit a world of increasing rights and recognition (Hammack & Cohler, 2011). The dominant cultural narrative of an
acceptable adult life in many nations has expanded to include lesbian, gay,
bisexual, and transgendered (LGBT) individuals. While LGBTs continue to
experience discrimination and harassment in many nations, in the United
States and elsewhere a master narrative of sickness and deviance has given
way to the idea of sexual and gender identity diversity as "normative" facts
of social and cultural life (Cohler & Hammack, 2007; Hammack, Mayers,
& Windell, 2013). A heterosexual union is no longer considered inevitable,
and the intrinsic link between adulthood and heterosexuality has eroded to
accommodate sexual and gender identity diversity in the 21st century. With
this cultural shift, the process of human development through engagement
with master narratives of social categories suggests new possibilities for self-
understanding in adulthood (Hammack & Cohler, 2009). Cohler's (1982)
idea of human development as a process of *interpretive activity*, always situated in a particular time and place, is illustrated.

In this chapter, we revisit Cohler's (1982) theoretical treatise on personal narrative and life course, with a focus on its implications for the social construction of adulthood in the 21st century. We develop three points
of elaboration and expansion. First, we highlight the radicalism in Cohler's
(1982) commitment to a person-centered approach to the study of lives
that, with its idiographic foundation (Allport, 1937), challenges the essen-
tialism inherent in much research in personality and social psychology, particularly with regard to social categories (Gjerde, 2004; Reicher & Hopkins,
2001).

NEW DIRECTIONS FOR CHILD AND ADOLESCENT DEVELOPMENT • DOI: 10.1002/cad

Second, we expand upon Cohler's (1982) idea of human development as a process of reconstructive activity conducted through personal narrative. We link Cohler's (1982) approach, originally anchored in psychoanalytic theory, to Vygotsky's (1978) cultural-historical activity theory (CHAT). We suggest that a key addition to Cohler's (1982) theoretical approach requires the examination of the link between what Vygotsky (1978) calls *social speech* and *inner speech* and what we call *master narratives* and *personal narratives* (see also Hammack, 2008, 2011a, 2011b). The result is a process of *narrative engagement* (Hammack & Cohler, 2009), rather than *personal narrative construction*, which better describes the dynamic, dialogic process through which reconstructive, interpretive activity occurs.

Finally, we highlight Cohler's (1982) *life course* or *sociogenic* perspective on human development (see also Dannefer, 1984; Elder, 1998) suggesting that adulthood represents a cultural discourse always associated with historical time and place (see also Schiff, Chapter 1 of this volume). We suggest that the contemporary discourse on adulthood in the 21st century in much of the world is linked to the larger social and economic context of late capitalism and globalization (e.g., Arnett, 2002) and that the meaning of adulthood has shifted considerably since the writing of Cohler's (1982) essay. The emergence of a newly demarcated period in the life course, *emerging adulthood* (Arnett, 2000, 2004), reveals the social construction of adulthood. We posit that narrative processes in emerging adulthood are key to the social construction of memory and identity, with implications for both individual development and social stasis and change.

## Narrative as Interpretive Activity

The sense of stability and consistency which is experienced over time results primarily from continuing reconstructive activity leading to the maintenance of a particular personal narrative of the life course, rather than a consequence of constancy of development. (Cohler, 1982, p. 205)

In our theoretical expansion of Cohler's (1982) concept of personal narrative, we first highlight the radical potential of his original theory for the study of lives. We then link his perspective to the CHAT approach to human development. This expansion is consistent with Cohler's later work in which he sought to link personal narratives of gay identity to social practice (e.g., Cohler, 2007; Cohler & Hammack, 2006).

First, Cohler's (1982) call for an interpretive approach to the study of lives presents a radical challenge to psychological and developmental science, both at the time of his writing and today (McAdams, Chapter 5 of this volume; Schiff, Chapter 1 of this volume). In contrast to perspectives on human development which emphasized normative sequences of "ages and stages" (e.g., Piaget, 1933/1954), Cohler (1982) redefined human development as a process of personal narrative construction across the life course. Individuals make meaning of life events, including events linked to biological maturation and social processes, by constructing a coherent story with an intelligible timeline (i.e., a beginning, middle, and end; see Habermas & Hatiboğlu, Chapter 3 of this volume; McAdams, Chapter 5 of this volume) and content linked to "socially shared definitions" (p. 205). "The personal narrative which is recounted at any point in the course of life represents the most internally consistent interpretation of presently understood past, experienced present, and anticipated future at that time" (p. 207).

According to Cohler (1982), the study of personal narrative development across the life course represents a more appropriate approach to the study of lives since it more closely interrogates lived experience in contrast to positivist approaches to the study of personality: "This interpretive approach to the study of the person parallels the approach actually used by persons in the successive interpretations or reconstructions of their own history as a personal narrative across the course of life" (p. 229). The conception of human development as a process of narrative meaning making reveals the dynamic, unpredictable nature of development and challenges the idea of normativity itself (see also McAdams, Chapter 5 of this volume; Schiff, Chapter 1 of this volume), as well as framing development in terms of narrative practices (Miller, Chen, & Olivarez, Chapter 2 of this volume) rather than particular "outcomes." This approach thus reverses the relationship between scientific discourse and lived experience, with the former derived from the latter.

The liberatory effect of this move, and of a more interpretive approach to the study of lives in general, is significant. Rather than social categories and their associated normative expectations reifying experience (Reicher & Hopkins, 2001), lived experience itself informs our understanding of both social categories and developmental processes more broadly. This interpretive approach reverses the historic hegemony associated with an ontogenetic approach to human development (Dannefer, 1984), in which lived experience is discarded and a disembodied subject is placed within established aggregate frameworks (e.g., traits; see Mishler, 1996). Particularly for individuals inhabiting social categories of historic subordination or exclusion (e.g., racial and sexual minorities, women), this reversal of scientific analysis from "top-down" to "bottom-up" is significant because scientists no longer collude in the reification of social categories but rather are able to critically interrogate social categorization itself as a process of power and control (see Reicher & Hopkins, 2001). Cohler's (1982) interpretive stance toward human development also provides a link to contemporaneous moves in anthropology, sociology, and cultural studies that emphasized meaning and context in human action (e.g., Geertz, 1973; Rabinow & Sullivan, 1987; Ricoeur, 1984). Thus, Cohler's (1982) approach sought to link the study of lives more directly to fields of knowledge production concerned less with prediction and control than with human understanding (see Bruner, 1990).

Our second point of elaboration and theoretical expansion centers on Cohler's (1982) notion of the personal narrative not as a "product" of human development but rather as a process of ongoing "reconstructive activity" (p. 205). This view of narrative reveals an alignment between Cohler and theorists in the CHAT tradition such as Vygotsky and Bakhtin. Vygotsky (1978) challenged the dominant view in developmental science of sequential stages, instead positing that development proceeds through mediated social practice—activity that occurs in a particular cultural environment and relies upon the material world of the developing person (e.g., cultural tools, including language). Vygotsky's (1934/1962) view on language as itself a form of social practice has a direct link to Cohler's (1982) narrative theory, as Vygotsky argues that *internalization of speech* represents psychological activity that guides development. According to Vygotsky, we develop *inner speech* through this process, and this inner speech can be conceptualized as a process of personal narrative construction, since that speech often assumes a narrative form.

Cohler (1982) importantly notes that personal narratives are formed in relation to "socially shared definitions," a claim that calls attention to another aspect of Vygotsky's (1978) CHAT that emphasizes the idea of *social speech*. Vygotsky and other theorists associated with CHAT (e.g., Bakhtin, 1981) highlight the way in which language is always tied to the ideological positions of a particular verbal community. In Bakhtin's (1981) words, "Language is not a neutral medium that passes freely and easily into the private property of the speaker's intentions; it is populated—overpopulated—with the intentions of others" (p. 294). Similar to Foucault's (1980) views on discourse and power, CHAT theorists view language as inherently politicized, always possessing implications for an existing configuration of power in society. The process of *appropriation* (Bakhtin, 1981) or *internalization* (Vygotsky, 1978) is thus not simply personal but rather fundamentally political in its link to power relations.

To provide a concrete example, Hammack (2011a) has illustrated how the personal narratives of Israelis and Palestinians appropriate elements of master narratives of identity that reproduce the stalemate of conflict between them. Jewish Israeli youth construct personal narratives that assume a redemptive form (McAdams & Bowman, 2001) and thematic content associated with historic persecution and victimization, contemporary existential insecurity, exceptionalism, and delegitimization of Palestinians (Hammack, 2011a). Palestinian youth construct personal narratives that assume a contaminated (McAdams & Bowman, 2001) or tragic form and thematic content associated with collective loss and land dispossession, contemporary existential insecurity, resistance, and delegitimization of Zionism (Hammack, 2011a). The voices of young Palestinians and Israelis are "populated," to use Bakhtin's (1981) term, with the intentions of others.

Personal narrative as human activity is hence best understood as a social process of dynamic engagement with existing tools, gestures, and symbolic forms such as language, all of which are tied to ideological positions and bring implications not just for individual development but also for history and politics.

Linking Cohler's (1982) narrative theory to CHAT allows us to theorize a process of *narrative engagement* (Hammack, 2011b; Hammack & Cohler, 2009) in which narrative is conceptualized not as a product of human development but as a form of situated activity in line with Cohler's (1982) original proposition. The idea of narrative engagement highlights the ongoing negotiation between social speech and inner speech that may be accessible but highly variable at different moments in a person's life, depending upon social, historical, and biological events that may not, as Cohler (1982) argues, assume a predictable pattern. The point is to interrogate this process as it occurs and to derive insights into human development that recognize the significance of context and meaning, rather than to derive a set of lawful regularities associated with the decontextualized aims of a positivist, rather than interpretive, human science (Hammack, 2011b; see also Rabinow & Sullivan, 1987).

In Cohler's (2007) later work examining the personal narratives of distinct generation cohorts of gay men, he adopts this theoretical view of personal narratives as linked to social practice and to master narratives of gay identity circulating at the time of development. For example, gay men like Duberman, born in the 1930s, constructed personal narratives in early adulthood characterized by the internalization of stigma, whereas gay men born in the 1940s and 1950s engaged with a narrative of gay liberation and new forms of social practice that resulted in distinct processes of personal narrative development (Cohler, 2007; Hammack & Cohler, 2011). These narratives have implications for history and politics, as new generations of LGBTs engage with discourses that challenge existing sexual and gender identity categories (e.g., Cohler & Hammack, 2007; Hammack, Thompson, & Pilecki, 2009). An important expansion of Cohler's (1982) original theory, then, centers on the significance of master narratives in the interpretive activity of personal narrative development.

We have identified two points of theoretical expansion of Cohler's (1982) original position on personal narratives. First, we suggested that the emphasis on interrogation of lived experience has the potential to reverse the relationship between positivist developmental science and the meaning-making process of human lives. Rather than reifying social categories and human traits by imposing the lens of these concepts on lives in progress, Cohler's (1982) interpretive approach suggests that we derive our understanding of categories of human understanding from the active process of personal narration. Second, we suggested that Cohler's (1982) interpretive approach relies upon a view of development through mediated activity, chiefly engagement with the discourse and language existing in a particular verbal community at a particular historical moment. As individuals appropriate or repudiate existing forms of discourse through their ongoing reconstructive activity, they participate in a larger process of social reproduction or change, always with implications for an existing configuration of power in society. This idea represents a strong subtext within Cohler's (1982) original essay, which focuses decidedly more on the person than on society, but an explicit link to social theory that emphasizes language, discourse, and power enhances the theoretical vision and speaks to his later work on gay identity (e.g., Cohler, 2007).

## Adulthood in Social and Historical Time

> Assumption of adult roles provides the possibility for further elaboration of the personal narrative, as transformed through the resolution of the identity crisis of adolescence. The elements of this narrative are tested, in particular, by the assumption of parenthood. (Cohler, 1982, p. 221)

A narrative approach to the study of lives suggests not only that individual lives are based upon ongoing interpretive activity, but also that the human life course is itself a matter of collective interpretive activity. Hence, the very ideas of *childhood, adolescence,* or *adulthood* represent discourses of human interpretation. The meaning of these moments in the life span is socially situated and varies across time and place (e.g., Aries, 1960/1962; Elder, 1974; Erikson, 1950; Kett, 1977; Lieblich, Chapter 6 of this volume; Neugarten, 1996). Our third point of elaboration centers on Cohler's (1982) commitment to a *life course* perspective on human development which views lives as intimately linked to cultural, historic, and economic contexts (e.g., Elder, 1974; see Schiff, Chapter 1 of this volume). We suggest that adulthood itself ought, through this theoretical lens, to be conceived not as an inevitable moment of biological maturation but rather as a social and cultural discourse to which individuals orient their personal narratives.

Strongly influenced by Elder (1974) and Neugarten (1979), Cohler (1982) situates his theory in the *life course,* rather than traditional *life span,* perspective in developmental science (see Elder, 1998). The life span paradigm traditionally associated with developmental psychology takes an *ontogenetic* perspective emphasizing individual processes with only a superficial account of context (Dannefer, 1984). A *sociogenic* perspective accords more weight to context and to the self-society link (Dannefer, 1984). Cohler's (1982) life course approach is consistent with a sociogenic perspective that recognizes adulthood not as a biological phenomenon of aging but as a form of human social organization intended to provide both intelligibility for individual lives and a mechanism for social reproduction. Hence,

Cohler's (1982) account places matters of history and historical timing at the center.

The life course is therefore a matter of ongoing interpretation, as the social and economic needs of societies shift with human invention and cultural practices (e.g., Dannefer, 2003). With the rise of industrialism came a longer period of delay for entry into the workforce, a subsequent longer period of schooling, and the establishment of the concept of *adolescence* as its own distinct life stage marking the transition between childhood and adulthood (Kett, 1977). The meaning of adulthood has also shifted radically with social and economic change, with the nature of late capitalism characterized by an even longer period of delay for entry into certain forms of labor involved in an information-based economy (Arnett, 2000; Shanahan, 2000). These social and economic shifts have resulted in another new stage of the life course dubbed *emerging adulthood* (Arnett, 2000, 2004, 2011). Emerging adulthood represents a period in which many in postindustrial societies extend their education and delay milestones that previously occurred at younger ages, such as marriage and parenthood. Rather than identity being "resolved" or "achieved" at the end of adolescence (Cohler, 1982; Erikson, 1950), it remains an ongoing project, assuming significance in emerging adulthood as matters of love, work, and social position assume prominence (Arnett, 2004).

Our point here is that adulthood, like all periods of the human life course, represents a cultural discourse that impinges upon the individual's ongoing process of reconstructive activity in the personal narrative. Here, we expand upon Cohler's (1982) discussion of adulthood, which has relatively little to say about the personal narrative in adulthood beyond the significance of parenthood, to suggest that the very idea of adulthood and adult status in a society is associated with normative roles and expectations that command particular forms of generativity—namely contributions to a capitalist economy and, to a somewhat lessening extent in some cultural contexts, compulsory heterosexuality and reproduction. In other words, the master narrative of adulthood with which many in the postindustrial world engage is one that encourages practices associated with reproduction of a social and economic status quo, with little attention to issues of inequality.

The proliferation of this hegemonic master narrative of adulthood is probably most visible when examining its moments of challenge. Examples include social movements such as the "Occupy" movement that involved many emerging adults challenging the economic status quo (Gitlin, 2012) and the LGBT movement's push for marriage, which alters the link among traditional adult roles, institutions, and heterosexuality. Although hegemonic discourses on the nature and meaning of adulthood continue to exist, these examples of protest reveal the way in which master narratives are in constant states of tension and renegotiation, as individuals do not blindly internalize them but rather *engage* with them (Cohler & Hammack, 2007).

NEW DIRECTIONS FOR CHILD AND ADOLESCENT DEVELOPMENT • DOI: 10.1002/cad

In many ways, Cohler's (1982) views on narrative in adulthood are the least radical in his original essay, for they present a view of adulthood that is anchored in compulsory heterosexuality (a view from which he would later depart; e.g., Cohler, 2006) and traditional roles. The liberatory potential of Cohler's (1982) original ideas, though, can be realized in the recognition that adulthood itself represents not a moment of inevitable social and biological processes but rather a cultural discourse in relation to which lives are interpreted and positioned. The empirical concern then becomes an interrogation of how individuals negotiate master narratives as they construct coherent and purposive personal narratives.

## Narrative and Identity in Emerging Adulthood

...What young adults set out to do in the way of identity construction is...elicited by and subject to the responses and interests of their social worlds. (Pasupathi, 2001, p. 666)

The main psychosocial task of emerging adulthood is to author a narrative identity. (McAdams & Olson, 2010, p. 534)

If adulthood represents a discourse in relation to which lives are positioned, what narrative processes are particularly relevant to emerging adulthood? Emerging adulthood represents a time in which individuals in many nations negotiate not only the meaning of their identities in relation to their personal past and present, but also make meaning of the very idea of adulthood by reproducing or challenging existing cultural scripts inherited from past generations. In other words, narrative processes in emerging adulthood represent a critical turning point for both the individual and society, as the person situates himself or herself as a cultural participant with implications for either the reproduction or repudiation of a status quo. The ongoing reconstructive activity of narrative in emerging adulthood thus involves two critical functions: (a) the coconstruction of identity and memory through situated storytelling and (b) the individual construction of a life story that provides a sense of personal and social meaning in relation to society.

As a time defined by transition, emerging adulthood is marked by disruptive and self-defining experiences and the formation of new intimate relationships (Pasupathi, 2001). Sharing situated stories is a way for emerging adults to dialogically coconstruct the meaning of these experiences and develop or maintain their identities (McLean, Pasupathi, & Pals, 2007). A well-established line of research in this area has revealed the important role of social and cultural context, goals, and listeners in storytelling (e.g., McLean & Pasupathi, 2011; see Thorne & Nam, 2009). These studies suggest that listeners help to impart meaning to stories, influence how

NEW DIRECTIONS FOR CHILD AND ADOLESCENT DEVELOPMENT • DOI: 10.1002/cad

elaborately they are told, and how well they are remembered (Pasupathi & Hoyt, 2009; Thorne, McLean, & Lawrence, 2004). Emerging adults most commonly report telling stories to peers (as opposed to parents, as in early adolescence; McLean, 2005) for self-related functions (as opposed to older adults, who more often tell stories for social functions; McLean & Lilgendahl, 2008). This research reveals narrative as situated activity either implicitly or explicitly linked to the notion of development as a process of ongoing social practice (e.g., Vygotsky, 1978). Thus, narrative represents the tool through which the past is socially constructed (Pasupathi, 2001). Although research conducted in this approach highlights the active, dialogic process of personal narrative associated with Cohler's (1982) original views, it departs from his vision in a key way: The methodological emphasis on narrative as disembodied speech effectively erases the person as an active, agentic subject. Narrative data in these studies are aggregated across persons, and a positivist, rather than interpretive, approach to data analysis is employed. This aggregated, nomothetic approach to data analysis neglects personal meaning and lived experience—central aspects of Cohler's (1982) theoretical position.

A second function of narrative in emerging adulthood is to provide an interpretive anchor for an individual's navigation of the social world, which occurs through the construction of a life story (McAdams & Olson, 2010). Research consistent with Cohler's (1982) interpretive approach reveals the way in which individuals engage with multiple discourses as they construct coherent personal narratives. Schachter's (2004) research with Jewish Israeli Orthodox emerging adults interrogates the way in which individuals reconcile multiple and conflicting discourses of religion and sexuality. Gregg's (2007) work with young Moroccans illustrates the way in which they engage with conflicting discourses of tradition and modernity in the larger cultural context of economic underdevelopment as they narrate their life stories. Schiff's (2002) research with Arab emerging adults in Jerusalem illustrates the significance of social relationships in "identity talk," revealing the dialogic nature of personal narrative construction. Hammack and colleagues' (2009) work on sexual identity among U.S. emerging adults reveals the way in which they engage with competing narratives of the meaning of same-sex attraction as they construct life stories. These empirical examples illustrate how an interpretive, idiographic approach to narrative identity can reveal the ways in which emerging adults across cultural contexts engage in processes of social stasis and change as they reconcile conflicting discourses about religion, sexuality, nationality, and other social categories. They illustrate the way in which narrative processes in emerging adulthood have potential impact on historical and political processes. Research in this area that takes an interpretive focus adheres to Cohler's (1982) approach to the study of lives but expands his approach to take cultural variability into greater account.

# Conclusion

The guiding premise of social constructionism is that all aspects of material and psychological reality are the products of human invention (e.g., Gergen, 1999). The world is not merely "given" but rather "made" through ongoing human activity. Social constructionists place particular emphasis on the way in which language and language practices make and remake the social world, constructing forms of human intelligibility and establishing a particular social order (e.g., Berger & Luckmann, 1966).

Cohler's (1982) pathbreaking essay on personal narrative and life course can be interpreted as a treatise on the social construction of human development, and it provides a blueprint to study the dynamic link between self and society. In this chapter, we have highlighted three points of elaboration and theoretical expansion, and we have suggested that narrative processes in emerging adulthood assume a role in social stasis and change. Through the lens of social constructionism, adulthood is not simply a stage of human development. Rather, it represents a cultural and historical discourse toward which individuals orient their personal narratives through the ongoing interpretive activity of narrative engagement (Hammack & Cohler, 2009). Adulthood represents a form of social speech which individuals navigate as they undergo biological maturation and social experience, always contingent on a particular time and place. In this view, human development does not "unfold" in a particular predictable pattern but rather represents a dynamic process in which persons and contexts are dynamically coconstituted through the practices of language, including narrative engagement and personal narrative construction.

Cohler's (1982) essay was part of a revolution in psychology and developmental science that challenged the positivist, ontogenetic epistemology of the field. His theoretical stance on personal narrative and life course suggests that the study of adult development place central weight on the social context and historical timing of lives (see also Habermas & Hatiboğlu, Chapter 3 of this volume). Thus, social history and generation cohort likely assume significant roles in individual interpretive processes. We have expanded upon Cohler's (1982) theory to suggest that adulthood represents a master narrative against which individuals discursively position their own personal narratives in the ongoing reconstructive activity of narrative engagement. In other words, the expectations and possibilities of an adult life, whether in terms of relational or occupational possibilities, are tied to social, cultural, and economic conditions of a particular time and place. The narrative study of adult lives benefits from this social constructionist lens on adult development, providing insights not only into individual lives but also larger social processes of stasis and change.

Research that embraces the radical implications of Cohler's (1982) theory has gradually emerged, even if often not recognizing his contribution. To some extent, however, such work has been limited because of the continued hegemony of positivist approaches in psychological and developmental science that privilege quantification, aggregation, prediction, and control. Cohler's (1982) concern to interrogate the active process of meaning making and lived experience positions him within the move toward interpretive social science (Rabinow & Sullivan, 1987) and toward an approach to human development sensitive to history, politics, and culture. His pioneering essay warrants its place in the canon of narrative theory and humanistic approaches to social science research.

## References

Allport, G. W. (1937). *Personality: A psychological introduction*. New York, NY: Holt.

Aries, P. (1962). *Centuries of childhood: A social history of family life* (R. Baldick, Trans.). New York, NY: Vintage. (Original work published 1960)

Arnett, J. J. (2000). Emerging adulthood: A theory of development from the late teens through the twenties. *American Psychologist, 55*(5), 469–480.

Arnett, J. J. (2002). The psychology of globalization. *American Psychologist, 57,* 774–783.

Arnett, J. J. (2004). *Emerging adulthood: The winding road from the late teens through the twenties*. New York, NY: Oxford University Press.

Arnett, J. J. (2011). Emerging adulthood(s): The cultural psychology of a new life stage. In L. Jensen (Ed.), *Bridging cultural and developmental approaches to psychology: New syntheses in theory, research, and policy* (pp. 255–275). New York, NY: Oxford University Press.

Bakhtin, M. M. (1981). *The dialogic imagination* (C. Emerson & M. Holquist, Trans.). Austin: University of Texas Press.

Berger, P. L., & Luckmann, T. (1966). *The social construction of reality: A treatise in the sociology of knowledge*. New York, NY: Anchor.

Bruner, J. (1990). *Acts of meaning*. Cambridge, MA: Harvard University Press.

Cohler, B. J. (1982). Personal narrative and life course. In P. Baltes & O. G. Brim (Eds.), *Life span development and behavior* (Vol. 4, pp. 205–241). New York, NY: Academic Press.

Cohler, B. J. (2006). Life-course social science perspectives on the GLBT family. In J. J. Bigner (Ed.), *An introduction to GLBT family studies* (pp. 23–49). New York, NY: Haworth.

Cohler, B. J. (2007). *Writing desire: Sixty years of gay autobiography*. Madison: University of Wisconsin Press.

Cohler, B. J., & Hammack, P. L. (2006). Making a gay identity: Life story and the construction of a coherent self. In D. P. McAdams, R. Josselson, & A. Lieblich (Eds.), *Identity and story: Creating self in narrative* (pp. 151–172). Washington, DC: American Psychological Association Press.

Cohler, B. J., & Hammack, P. L. (2007). The psychological world of the gay teenager: Social change, narrative, and "normality." *Journal of Youth and Adolescence, 36,* 47–59.

Dannefer, D. (1984). Adult development and social theory: A paradigmatic reappraisal. *American Sociological Review, 49,* 100–116.

Dannefer, D. (2003). Toward a global geography of the life course: Challenges of late modernity for life course theory. In J. T. Mortimer & M. J. Shanahan (Eds.), *Handbook of the life course* (pp. 647–659). New York, NY: Kluwer.

Duberman, M. (1991). *Cures: A gay man's odyssey*. New York, NY: Dutton.

Duberman, M. (1993). *Stonewall*. New York, NY: Dutton.

Elder, G. H. (1974). *Children of the great depression: Social change in life experience*. Chicago, IL: University of Chicago Press.

Elder, G. H. (1998). The life course as developmental theory. *Child Development*, 69, 1–12.

Erikson, E. H. (1950). *Childhood and society*. New York, NY: Norton.

Foucault, M. (1980). *Power/knowledge: Selected interviews and other writings, 1972–1977*. New York, NY: Pantheon.

Geertz, C. (1973). *The interpretation of cultures*. New York, NY: Basic Books.

Gergen, K. J. (1999). *An invitation to social construction*. Thousand Oaks, CA: Sage.

Gitlin, T. (2012). *Occupy nation: The roots, the spirit, and the promise of Occupy Wall Street*. New York, NY: Harper Collins.

Gjerde, P. F. (2004). Culture, power, and experience: Toward a person-centered cultural psychology. *Human Development*, 47, 138–157.

Gregg, G. S. (2007). *Culture and identity in a Muslim society*. New York, NY: Oxford University Press.

Hammack, P. L. (2008). Narrative and the cultural psychology of identity. *Personality and Social Psychology Review*, 12(3), 222–247.

Hammack, P. L. (2011a). *Narrative and the politics of identity: The cultural psychology of Israeli and Palestinian youth*. New York, NY: Oxford University Press.

Hammack, P. L. (2011b). Narrative and the politics of meaning. *Narrative Inquiry*, 21(2), 311–318.

Hammack, P. L., & Cohler, B. J. (2009). Narrative engagement and sexual identity: An interdisciplinary approach to the study of sexual lives. In P. L. Hammack & B. J. Cohler (Eds.), *The story of sexual identity: Narrative perspectives on the gay and lesbian life course* (pp. 3–22). New York, NY: Oxford University Press.

Hammack, P. L., & Cohler, B. J. (2011). Narrative, identity, and the politics of exclusion: Social change and the gay and lesbian life course. *Sexuality Research and Social Policy*, 8, 162–182.

Hammack, P. L., Mayers, L., & Windell, E. P. (2013). Narrative, psychology, and the politics of sexual identity in the United States: From "sickness" to "species" to "subject." *Psychology & Sexuality*, 4(3), 219–243.

Hammack, P. L., Thompson, E. M., & Pilecki, A. (2009). Configurations of identity among sexual minority youth: Context, desire, and narrative. *Journal of Youth and Adolescence*, 38, 867–883.

Kett, J. F. (1977). *Rites of passage: Adolescence in America, 1790 to the present*. New York, NY: Basic Books.

McAdams, D. P., & Bowman, P. J. (2001). Narrating life's turning points: Redemption and contamination. In D. P. McAdams, R. Josselson, & A. Lieblich (Eds.), *Turns in the road: Narrative studies of lives in transition* (pp. 3–34). Washington, DC: American Psychological Association Press.

McAdams, D. P., & Olson, B. D. (2010). Personality development: Continuity and change over the life course. *Annual Review of Psychology*, 61, 517–542.

McLean, K. C. (2005). Late adolescent identity development: Narrative meaning making and memory telling. *Developmental Psychology*, 41(4), 683–691.

McLean, K. C., & Lilgendahl, J. P. (2008). Why recall our highs and lows: Relations between memory functions, age, and well-being. *Memory*, 16(7), 751–762.

McLean, K. C., & Pasupathi, M. (2011). Old, new, borrowed, blue? The emergence and retention of personal meaning in autobiographical storytelling. *Journal of Personality*, 79(1), 135–164.

McLean, K. C., Pasupathi, M., & Pals, J. L. (2007). Selves creating stories creating selves: A process model of self-development. *Personality and Social Psychology Review*, 11(3), 262–278.

Mishler, E. G. (1996). Missing persons: Recovering developmental stories/histories. In R. Jessor, A. Colby, & R. A. Shweder (Eds.), *Ethnography and human development:*

*Context and meaning in social inquiry* (pp. 73–100). Chicago, IL: University of Chicago Press.

Neugarten, B. (1979). Time, age, and the life cycle. *American Journal of Psychiatry, 136,* 887–894.

Neugarten, B. (1996). *The meanings of age: Selected papers.* Chicago, IL: University of Chicago Press.

Pasupathi, M. (2001). The social construction of the personal past and its implications for adult development. *Psychological Bulletin, 127*(5), 651–672.

Pasupathi, M., & Hoyt, T. (2009). The development of narrative identity in late adolescence and emergent adulthood: The continued importance of listeners. *Developmental Psychology, 45*(2), 558–574.

Piaget, J. (1933/1954). *The construction of reality in the child.* New York, NY: Basic Books.

Rabinow, P., & Sullivan, W. M. (Eds.). (1987). *Interpretive social science: A second look.* Berkeley: University of California Press.

Reicher, S., & Hopkins, N. (2001). Psychology and the end of history: A critique and proposal for the psychology of social categorization. *Political Psychology, 22*(2), 383–407.

Ricoeur, P. (1984). *Time and narrative* (Vol. 1; K. McLaughlin & D. Pellauer, Trans.). Chicago, IL: University of Chicago Press.

Schachter, E. P. (2004). Identity configurations: A new perspective on identity formation in contemporary society. *Journal of Personality, 72*(1), 167–200.

Schiff, B. (2002). Talking about identity: Arab students at the Hebrew University of Jerusalem. *Ethos, 30*(3), 273–304.

Shanahan, M. J. (2000). Pathways to adulthood in changing societies: Variability and mechanisms in life course perspective. *Annual Review of Sociology, 26,* 667–692.

Thorne, A., McLean, K. C., & Lawrence, A. M. (2004). When remembering is not enough: Reflecting on self-defining memories in late adolescence. *Journal of Personality, 72*(3), 513–541.

Thorne, A., & Nam, V. (2009). The storied construction of personality. In P. Corr & G. Matthews (Eds.), *Cambridge handbook of personality* (pp. 491–505). Cambridge, UK: Cambridge University Press.

Vygotsky, L. S. (1962). *Thought and language* (E. Hanfmann & G. Vakar, Trans.). Cambridge, MA: MIT Press. (Original work published 1934)

Vygotsky, L. S. (1978). *Mind in society: The development of higher psychological processes.* Cambridge, MA: Harvard University Press.

PHILLIP L. HAMMACK *is an associate professor of psychology at the University of California, Santa Cruz.*

ERIN TOOLIS *is a graduate student in social psychology at the University of California, Santa Cruz.*

NEW DIRECTIONS FOR CHILD AND ADOLESCENT DEVELOPMENT • DOI: 10.1002/cad

# The Life Narrative at Midlife

*Dan P. McAdams*

## Abstract

*In a remarkably prescient chapter, Bertram Cohler (1982) reimagined the problems and the potentialities of psychological development across the life course as a distinctively human challenge in life narration. This chapter situates Cohler's original vision within the intellectual and scientific matrix of the late 1970s, wherein psychologists expressed grave doubts about the extent to which human lives may demonstrate consistency and coherence. By focusing attention on human beings as autobiographical authors rather than as mere social actors or motivated agents, Cohler moved the conversation away from dispositional personality traits and developmental stages and toward the emerging concept of narrative identity. Over the past 30 years, research on narrative identity has shown how people use stories to integrate the reconstructed past and imagined future, providing their lives with some semblance of unity, purpose, and meaning. At midlife, many adults struggle to solve the problem of generativity, aiming to leave a positive legacy for the next generation. Inspired by Cohler's original chapter, contemporary research reveals that the most generative adults in American society tend to construe their lives as narratives of personal redemption. As such, life stories may serve as valuable psychological resources for midlife adults, even as they reflect and refract prevailing cultural themes. © 2014 Wiley Periodicals, Inc.*

NEW DIRECTIONS FOR CHILD AND ADOLESCENT DEVELOPMENT, no. 145, Fall 2014 © 2014 Wiley Periodicals, Inc.
Published online in Wiley Online Library (wileyonlinelibrary.com). • DOI: 10.1002/cad.20067

In one of the most perceptive and prescient chapters ever written in life span developmental psychology, Bert Cohler (1982) imagined human development as an ongoing narrative project. Human beings are storytellers of the self, Cohler (1982) asserted. Across countless interactions and over the long course of development, people construe their lives as integrative stories, complete with settings, scenes, characters, plots, and themes. Stories bring together the reconstructed past and the imagined future, and provide messy human lives with some semblance of meaning, order, and purpose. In that "lives are much less ordered and predictable than formerly recognized" by social scientists, people strive to "maintain an intelligible narrative over time," Cohler (1982, p. 210) suggested. When Cohler (1982) wrote *Personal Narrative and the Life Course*, developmental psychologists tended to conceive of human beings as (a) social *actors* who behave according to the role demands of human groups and (b) motivated *agents* who pursue personal goals and desires and aim to fulfill basic human needs. But Cohler (1982) turned their attention to the possibility that human beings are more than actors and agents. Humans are autobiographical *authors* too, and increasingly so as they move across the human life course.

## Actors, Agents, and Authors

Among the many intellectual problems that Bert Cohler (1982) sought to address in his visionary synthesis was a conundrum that vexed personality and developmental psychologists in the 1970s and early 1980s: *To what extent are human lives consistent and coherent?*

By the time Cohler wrote his chapter, many personality psychologists had lost faith in the idea that people behave in consistent ways across situations and over time as a function of their underlying dispositional traits. Reaching a crescendo in the late 1970s, the situationist critique argued against the efficacy of traits, even doubting that people possess internal and stable individual differences in personality (Mischel, 1968). To the extent that people show individual differences in behavior and emotion, the situationists argued, those differences are driven by the exigencies of social situations. As social actors, people mainly behave in accordance with situational demands and group norms.

Around the same time, many developmentalists were beginning to lose faith in the broad and integrative developmental claims made by stage theories, such as those proposed by Piaget, Kohlberg, and Erikson. Stage models sought to go beneath the surface of social action to expose underlying structures of motivation and cognition. For example, Erikson (1950) viewed human beings as motivated agents who seek to achieve developmentally appropriate goals, such as the goal of interpersonal trust (vs. mistrust—Stage 1 in Erikson's scheme) in infancy and the goal of intimacy (vs. isolation—Stage 6) in young adulthood. Rather than envisioning human development

NEW DIRECTIONS FOR CHILD AND ADOLESCENT DEVELOPMENT • DOI: 10.1002/cad

as an orderly unfolding of stages, however, psychologists in the late 1970s were beginning to appreciate how lives are rather more contingent and uneven than stage models would suggest. As motivated agents, people aim to achieve the goals that arise at any given moment in the life course as a function of that moment's exigencies. Changing life circumstances— unpredictable and serendipitous—trump normative developmental timetables.

For decades, then, the psychological constructs of dispositional *traits* and developmental *stages* had buttressed the conviction that human beings behave in characteristically consistent ways over time (as social actors) and that they pursue developmentally appropriate (stage-governed) aims and goals (as motivated agents). By 1980, however, these concepts had lost favor. Cohler (1982) accepted the prevailing critiques of traits and stages. Strongly influenced by perspectives from life-course sociology (e.g., Elder, 1975), he understood that human lives were complexly situated in culture and history, and subject to such unpredictable events as wars and recessions, changing personal circumstances, lucky breaks and personal tragedies, and everyday chance. In the midst of relentless social change and motivational unpredictability, however, people maintain a drive toward making meaning out of their lives, Cohler asserted. People perceive consistency and they create coherence, he argued, even if they do not behave in a trait-like manner and even if their own development fails to follow a predictable stage sequence. They perceive consistency and create coherence through *narrative*:

> Studies of lives have suggested that the course of development may be much less predictable and well-ordered than previously realized. Rather than viewing personality development either in terms of continuing stability over time or in terms of a number of well-ordered phases or stages, lives seem to be characterized by often abrupt transformations determined both by unexpected and eruptive life events and by intrinsic, but not necessarily continuous, developmental factors, including biological aging. These events taking place across the life course are later remembered as elements of a narrative which provides a coherent account of this often disjunctive life course. The form of this narrative is based upon a socially shared belief in Western culture that all narratives, including history, literature, and biography, must have a beginning, a middle, and an end related to each other in a meaningful manner. (Cohler, 1982, pp. 228–229)

Today, personality and developmental psychologists have recovered from the doubts they experienced in Cohler's (1982) days regarding the concept of the trait. Thirty years of research on child temperament and adult personality development have convincingly shown that dispositional dimensions (such as positive emotionality and effortful control in children, and extraversion and conscientiousness in adults) are powerful predictors of consistent behavioral and emotional trends in life, even as they change in response to social influences and gene by environment interactions (Caspi, Roberts, & Shiner, 2005). Contra the claims made by situationists in the 1970s, individual differences in dispositional traits show high levels of heritability, increasingly robust stability over the life course, and impressive connections to such valued life outcomes as mental health and well-being, delinquency and crime, occupational success, divorce, and longevity (Roberts, Kuncel, Shiner, Caspi, & Goldberg, 2007). From infancy onward, dispositional traits track broad consistencies in behavioral and emotional performance from the standpoint of the person as a social actor (McAdams & Olson, 2010).

From the perspective of the motivated agent, developmental psychologists are even more skeptical today than they were in 1982 regarding the viability of broad-based stage models. However, they have articulated a range of conceptions that underscore the role of goals, plans, values, and other agentic features of personality development (Mroczek & Little, 2006). Life may not unfold as a neat developmental sequence, but motivated agents often manage to cope and gain control over the unpredictable challenges they face. In many lives, agents make developmental progress in establishing, maintaining, and actualizing their respective motivational agendas (Mischel, 2004). As social actors express consistency in behavior across situations and over time, motivated agents also demonstrate some level of personality coherence in the goals and values they pursue. Therefore, the concerns regarding consistency and coherence, so pressing in the fields of personality and developmental psychology in 1982, have largely subsided. Part of the impetus for Cohler's (1982) proposal, therefore, is no longer relevant today.

But Cohler's (1982) take-home points regarding personal narrative could not be more germane three decades after he made them. The past 30 years have witnessed a remarkable upsurge of interest among social scientists in the idea of life narrative (e.g., Bamberg & Andrews, 2004; Josselson & Lieblich, 1993; Sarbin, 1986; Schiff, Chapter 1 of this volume). The turn toward narrative, both as a methodology for scientific inquiry and as an integrative conception for human lives, can be seen in fields as divergent as sociology, clinical psychology, and neuroscience. Within personality and developmental psychology, the central concept around which a great deal of theory and research revolves is *narrative identity* (McAdams, 1985; McAdams & McLean, 2013; Singer, 2004). Refining an idea that runs throughout Cohler's (1982) paper, contemporary personality and developmental psychologists define narrative identity as an internalized and evolving life story that reconstrues the autobiographical past and imagines the future in such a way as to affirm threads of continuity and coherence in a person's life. Human beings are social actors at birth, and they begin to articulate personal goals and values in their childhood years. But it is not until late adolescence and young adulthood that people begin to work on their narrative identities in full force, taking on the psychological perspective of the self-reflective autobiographical author (McAdams, 2013a).

The personal construction of narrative identity in late adolescence and beyond builds on the storytelling skills and inclinations that begin to emerge in childhood. By the time children reach what Cohler (1982) described as the *age 5–7 shift*, they have internalized conventional norms regarding how to translate personal experiences into coherent stories (Fivush, 2011; Mandler, 1984). They know, for example, that stories begin with a motivated protagonist (an agent) who wants something. The protagonist sets forth to accomplish his or her goal, but the pursuit of the goal meets some form of complication, be it an obstacle, a challenge, or an unexpected turn of events. A plot then develops, playing out across a temporal landscape of action and consciousness. The story finally ends with some sort of resolution to the tension that accompanied the goal pursuit in the first place. Whereas Cohler (1982) couched the early development of narrative inclinations in terms of Freud's conception of the Oedipus complex, contemporary researchers tend to focus on emerging cognitive skills (such as the ability to understand that other agents have minds containing desires and beliefs) and the everyday practice in storytelling that young children enjoy in conversations with parents, teachers, and peers (Fivush, 2011; Miller, Chen, & Olivarez, Chapter 2 of this volume).

Whereas grade-school children can tell coherent stories about their personal experiences, they do not yet see their full lives as ongoing narratives writ large, stories that they both work on (as narrators) and live out (as protagonists who pursue goals and make meaning over time). As Cohler (1982) suggested, adolescence ushers in a broader understanding of time and the life course, paving the way for narrative identity. "For the first time in the life course, the present is seen as situated between past and future," Cohler (1982, p. 218) wrote, in reference to adolescence. The autobiographical author now faces the challenge of reconstructing the past so that it connects in a meaningful way to what the future is anticipated to be.

Habermas and Bluck (2000) have shown that connecting the past to the future through narrative identity requires the actualization of a suite of cognitive and experiential facilities that do not typically come online until the adolescent years. For example, adolescents (but typically not children) are able to connect disparate personal events into causal chains in order to explain how they came to hold a particular point of view or express a particular characteristic of the self—a facility that Habermas and Bluck (2000) term *causal coherence*. Adolescents are also able to derive a theme or conclusion about the self from a set of exemplary life events, expressing *thematic coherence*. In everyday social interactions, adolescents and young adults draw upon increasingly sophisticated skills of autobiographical reasoning to share stories about their lives, editing and transforming their respective understandings of their lives in the process, as selves create stories which, in turn, create new selves (Habermas & Hatiboğlu, Chapter

3 of this volume; McLean, Pasupathi, & Pals, 2007). Over time, narrative identities emerge and take psychological hold, as authors articulate clearer, more coherent, and more convincing stories about how they have come to be the persons they are becoming.

## Narrative Identity in Midlife

In tracing the development of personal narratives over the life course, Cohler (1982) highlighted three developmental epochs. In the age 5–7 shift, children convey their subjective experiences through stories about desire, belief, and goals. They now feel that they are characters in a larger emotional drama, motivated agents who strive to fulfill their inner needs and wants. In adolescence, people take ownership of the dramas themselves. They become full-fledged autobiographical authors who create narrative identities as they live them out. For the third epoch, Cohler (1982) jumped ahead to *midlife*.

In the early 1980s, the idea of a *midlife crisis* was new and cutting-edge, and it stimulated a wealth of theorizing regarding the psychology of adult development (Jacques, 1965; Levinson, 1978). A major theme in this literature was that midlife ushered in an increasing awareness of life's finitude: "A major consequence of the attainment of midlife is the recognition that more than half of one's life may already have been lived," Cohler (1982, p. 223) wrote. "Such recognition leads to a foreshortened sense of the lifeline and, in turn, to increased awareness of mortality, or the finitude of life" (p. 223). As a result, midlife adults may become more introspective and reflective as they age. They may focus more attention on the past than they have before, Cohler (1982) suggested, serving to enrich their narrative identities and to reveal more nuanced understandings of the self. Indeed, contemporary research suggests that midlife adults engage in more sophisticated forms of autobiographical reasoning than do younger adults and adolescents, expressing deeper insights into how their life's journey has shaped who they are (Baddeley & Singer, 2007; Pasupathi & Mansour, 2006).

Moreover, Cohler (1982) argued that midlife adults tend to use personal narratives about the past "to solve problems in the present" (p. 224). Not only was Cohler one of the first psychologists to understand that people conceive of their lives in narrative form, but he also realized that people do so *for a purpose*. Life stories function to solve general identity problems for most people—the broad psychological problems regarding coherence and continuity in life. Stories tell us who we are, who we were, and who we will be. But stories also manage to address more particular problems that may arise at specific points in the life course. For example, young adults (and others) may use their stories to attract potential mates and establish intimacy with others. Parents may draw upon their own life stories to instruct their children in the ways of the world. For midlife adults, many of the greatest challenges in life may revolve around the issue of generativity,

or the concern for establishing, maintaining, and guiding the next generation. Erikson (1950) identified *generativity versus stagnation* as the central
developmental challenge for midlife adults. In their roles as parents, teachers, mentors, leaders, and stakeholders in society, midlife adults strive to
promote the well-being and success of younger people, those who will follow them in the sequence of generations. When midlife adults fail in this
task, as they often do, they may feel that their lives are stagnant, or they may
be so preoccupied with their own well-being that they cannot find space in
their lives to be of service to others.

How, then, do life stories help midlife adults solve the problem of generativity? This question has animated a line of research in personality and
developmental psychology that owes much of its inspiration to Cohler's
(1982) vision. Beginning with McAdams (1985), my own research on narrative identity has paid special attention to the life stories constructed by
especially generative midlife adults. How do the most generative adults in
society—caring and productive adults who are demonstrably committed to
promoting the well-being of future generations—make sense of their own
lives? Research conclusively shows that adults who score high on well-
validated measures of generativity tend to be involved in a wide range of
challenging life activities, as they commit themselves to making a positive
difference in the realms of family, church, community, politics, and society
writ large (McAdams, 2001; Rossi, 2001). While these commitments are
significant sources of fulfillment, they also bring with them more than a
fair share of frustration. Generativity is hard work. You need a good story
to get you through.

Findings from qualitative case studies and quantitative assessments of
life narrative protocols suggest that highly generative adults in American
society tend to construct their lives as narratives of personal *redemption*
(McAdams, 2013b; McAdams & de St. Aubin, 1992; McAdams, Diamond,
de St. Aubin, & Mansfield, 1997; McAdams, Reynolds, Lewis, Patten, &
Bowman, 2001; see also Colby & Damon, 1992; Walker & Frimer, 2007). In
redemptive life stories, the protagonist repeatedly encounters setbacks, failures, losses, and disappointments. But negative events are often redeemed
by positive outcomes as the protagonist continues to grow and prosper.

Redemptive life stories often begin with the protagonist experiencing
an early blessing or advantage. As the midlife narrator recalls childhood
today, he or she enjoyed a special status in the early years, perhaps an especially loving relationship with a relative or teacher, or a skill, talent, or
proclivity that distinguished the protagonist from others. At the same time,
the protagonist was especially cognizant of the misfortune of others. Compared to less generative adults, for example, adults scoring high on self-
report measures of generativity are about three times more likely to highlight early experiences of witnessing the suffering of others when telling
the stories of their lives. The stories implicitly suggest that the main character enjoys an early advantage in life while other characters in the story

may suffer greatly. The story suggests this: "I am blessed, but others suffer. I am the gifted protagonist who journeys forth into a dangerous world." Over the course of the redemptive narrative, the protagonist experiences pain and misfortune, too, but these negative events are often followed by positive outcomes, or else the protagonist gains insights and strength from suffering. Adversity is overcome, sins are washed away, what almost kills me makes me a stronger person in the long run. In gratitude for the blessings received and in response to the suffering witnessed in the lives of others, the protagonist resolves to leave a positive mark on the world, consolidating a commitment to future generations.

Redemptive life stories help to solve the problem of generativity by affirming the commitments and justifying the hard work that living a generative life entails. As an autobiographical author, the midlife adult recalls his or her own early blessings and the painful misfortunes of other people, suggesting that he or she has been called or mandated—by fate, luck, God, whatever—to live a life of service to others. Generativity becomes a kind of personal mission, justified in narrative by the early blessings received and the fact that the world needs you, for you are blessed and others suffer. Moreover, the burdens that come with generativity may seem lighter if one's story confirms the expectation that personal setbacks are often overcome, that suffering eventually gives way to enhancement, and that tough times today will result in prosperity and happiness tomorrow. For many generative adults, then, redemptive life stories serve as a psychological resource. They reinforce hope that generative investments will pay off in the long run, no matter how difficult and daunting the midlife challenge of generativity may appear to be.

The redemptive life stories told by highly generative midlife adults, as described in McAdams (2013b) and other places, also illustrate the power of *culture* in shaping the stories that people tell. For the most part, research on the life stories of highly generative adults has focused on *American* adults at midlife. The redemptive stories told by highly generative American adults evoke powerful metaphors and motifs that run through American culture, history, and heritage. As evidenced in popular fiction, television and movies, American religious traditions, and many other cultural expressions, Americans seem especially drawn to narratives of redemption. McAdams (2013b) identifies at least four canonical versions of redemptive stories that enjoy tremendous cachet in American history and in everyday discourse.

First, narratives of *atonement* track the move from sin to salvation, reflecting America's strong Protestant heritage and the worldviews of the Massachusetts Bay Puritans who came to the New World in the 17th century. A second line of redemptive narrative tracks the move from rags to riches, the stories of *upward social mobility* in the United States, canonized as the American Dream. A third line recalls stories of emancipation, as in the slave narratives of 19th century America, tracking the move from oppression to freedom. The same kinds of *liberation* stories have historically animated American social movements regarding civil rights, women's rights, and (most recently) the rights of gays and lesbians. Finally, narratives of *recovery* look backward to a golden age, a paradise lost that beckons to be refound, as in stories of recovery from illness, addiction, and abuse. Rising to fame shortly after Cohler (1982) published his classic chapter, Oprah Winfrey has probably been the most influential American spokesperson for narratives of recovery in the past 25 years, living a recovery story herself and teaching others how to understand their lives in the same way.

Culture provides a menu of images, metaphors, plots, and characters for the making of narrative identity. Autobiographical authors sample the menu that their culture presents them. They appropriate culturally valued narrative material in ways that capture, as well as contour, their own personal experiences. As Hammack (2008) has argued, culture presents autobiographical authors with *master narratives* over and against which one's personal identity may be compared (see also Hammack & Toolis, Chapter 4 of this volume; Rosenwald & Ochberg, 1992). American stories of atonement, upward mobility, liberation, and recovery may function as master narratives for many highly generative American adults, who find that their own experiences can be readily assimilated to a canonical redemptive form. But for many people, master narratives of culture may become objects of rejection or resistance. An autobiographical author may self-consciously construct a narrative identity that defies the conventions of a master narrative. The person may reject a master narrative because his or her own personal experiences may diverge dramatically from cultural expectations. Or the person may believe that cultural expectations are oppressive or immoral, serving to reinforce values that are contrary to what the person holds to be true and good. As Cohler (1982) recognized, personal narratives do not always line up nicely with the broader stories that may prevail in any given culture and at any particular historical moment. Authoring a life story is a tricky affair, a psychocultural activity of self-creation and re-creation, operating within the tense and dynamic space that lies between phenomenal experience and cultural reality.

## Conclusion

In his last paragraph, Cohler (1982) critiqued psychological science for its dependence upon the methods and models of the natural sciences. If people understand their own lives as ongoing narratives, Cohler reasoned, perhaps empirical psychologists themselves should revamp their research paradigms to accommodate the principles of narrative inquiry:

> Acceptance of the narrative approach means accepting a different criterion for judging the adequacy of scholarship in this field than has been used over the past several decades in the behavioral sciences. However, the narrative approach may be more appropriate for the subject being studied, and may

eventually provide better understanding of the factors shaping subjectively interpreted intents, than the explanatory models of the natural sciences. This interpretive approach to the study of the person parallels the approach usually used by persons in the successive interpretations or reconstructions of their own history as a personal narrative across the course of life. (Cohler, 1982, p. 229)

As Cohler (1982) saw it, it may not be enough for psychological scientists merely to recognize the importance of life stories and then subject this complex topic to conventional empirical scrutiny. Psychological scientists need to go one step further, Cohler said. They need to become storytellers themselves. They need to adopt the means and modes of life narration in the very act of studying how human beings narrate their lives (Freeman, Chapter 7 of this volume). Cohler's (1982) vision for a more interpretative science of persons was not new, of course. Wilhelm Dilthey (1900/1976) made much the same argument over 100 years ago, in imagining a hermeneutical human science, or what he called the *Geisteswissenschaften*. Since then, many other critics of conventional scientific practice have argued forcefully for a science of persons that is less reductionistic and mechanistic than what psychological scientists typically prefer, a science that privileges the subjective interpretations and interactions of the scientist himself or herself (Gergen, 1982; Stern, 1938).

These kinds of critiques picked up new steam in the 1980s and 1990s as advocates for narrative approaches reimagined psychological investigation as narrative inquiry (Polkinghorne, 1988; Shotter & Gergen, 1989). Indeed, Cohler's (1982) vision became partly realized in the rise of a strong interdisciplinary movement focused on *the narrative study of lives* (Josselson & Lieblich, 1993; McAdams, Josselson, & Lieblich, 2006). As a result, social scientists of many different stripes seem, over the past two decades, to have become more accepting of narrative approaches to research, especially when these approaches involve the collection of narrative data through structured interviews and open-ended questionnaire methods, and the use of validated content-analysis systems to code the data (McAdams, 2012). They also value narrative case studies and other purely qualitative expositions as vivid illustrations of theoretical ideas and vehicles for the discovery of new theory. Nonetheless, most researchers are reluctant to discard completely the canons of rigorous scientific inquiry, which include objective operationalization of variables, empirical hypothesis testing, and replicability of observations. It is not clear how far one should go in embracing a purely interpretive, narrative-based approach to the human sciences. Like other people, scientists may be storytellers. But good science, even good psychological science as applied to human lives, seems to rely on principles of inquiry that are somewhat different from those that make for a good story. This is to say that storytellers enjoy a certain kind of freedom that science typically forswears.

NEW DIRECTIONS FOR CHILD AND ADOLESCENT DEVELOPMENT • DOI: 10.1002/cad

Over the past 30 years, then, personality and developmental psychologists have adopted a range of conventional scientific methods to explore the life story at midlife. While they have not fully embraced Cohler's (1982) call for a radical rethinking of scientific methods themselves, researchers have made remarkable progress in making sense of how adults make narrative sense of their own lives. A full psychological understanding of adult lives at midlife requires a careful consideration of how midlife adults, as social actors, perform their daily roles; how they strive, as motivated agents, to attain their most cherished goals and values in the future; and how, as autobiographical authors of the self, midlife adults make meaning out of it all—past, present, and future—through life narrative.

## References

Baddeley, J., & Singer, J. A. (2007). Charting the life story's path: Narrative identity across the life span. In J. Chandinin (Ed.), *Handbook of narrative research methods* (pp. 177–202). Thousand Oaks, CA: Sage.

Bamberg, M. G. W., & Andrews, M. (Eds.). (2004). *Considering counter-narratives: Narrating, resisting, making sense*. Amsterdam, The Netherlands: John Benjamins.

Caspi, A., Roberts, B. W., & Shiner, R. L. (2005). Personality development: Stability and change. In S. T. Fiske & D. Schacter (Eds.), *Annual review of psychology* (Vol. 56, pp. 453–484). Palo Alto, CA: Annual Reviews.

Cohler, B. J. (1982). Personal narrative and life course. In P. B. Baltes & O. G. Brim (Eds.), *Life-span development and behavior* (Vol. 4, pp. 205–241). New York, NY: Academic Press.

Colby, A., & Damon, W. (1992). *Some do care: Contemporary lives of moral commitment.* New York, NY: The Free Press.

Dilthey, W. (1900/1976). The development of hermeneutics. In H. P. Rickman (Ed.), *W. Dilthey: Selected writings* (pp. 247–263). Cambridge, UK: Cambridge University Press.

Elder, G. (1975). Age differentiation and the life course. *Annual Review of Sociology, 1,* 165–190.

Erikson, E. H. (1950). *Childhood and society.* New York, NY: Norton.

Fivush, R. (2011). The development of autobiographical memory. In S. T. Fiske, D. L. Schacter, & S. E. Taylor (Eds.), *Annual review of psychology* (Vol. 62, pp. 550–582). Palo Alto, CA: Annual Reviews.

Gergen, K. J. (1982). *Toward transformation in social knowledge.* New York, NY: Springer.

Habermas, T., & Bluck, S. (2000). Getting a life: The emergence of the life story in adolescence. *Psychological Bulletin, 126,* 748–769.

Hammack, P. L. (2008). Narrative and the cultural psychology of identity. *Personality and Social Psychology Review, 12,* 222–247.

Jacques, E. (1965). Death and the midlife crisis. *International Journal of Psychoanalysis, 46,* 502–514.

Josselson, R., & Lieblich, A. (Eds.). (1993). *The narrative study of lives.* Thousand Oaks, CA: Sage.

Levinson, D. J. (1978). *The seasons of a man's life.* New York, NY: Alfred A. Knopf.

Mandler, J. (1984). *Stories, scripts, and scenes: Aspects of schema theory.* Hillsdale, NJ: Erlbaum.

McAdams, D. P. (1985). *Power, intimacy, and the life story: Personological inquiries into identity.* New York, NY: Guilford Press.

McAdams, D. P. (2001). Generativity in midlife. In M. E. Lachman (Ed.), *Handbook of midlife development* (pp. 395–443). New York, NY: Wiley.

McAdams, D. P. (2012). Exploring psychological themes through life narrative accounts. In J. A. Holstein & J. F. Gubrium (Eds.), *Varieties of narrative analysis* (pp. 15–32). London, UK: Sage.

McAdams, D. P. (2013a). The psychological self as actor, agent, and author. *Perspectives on Psychological Science, 8*, 272–295.

McAdams, D. P. (2013b). *The redemptive self: Stories Americans live by* (revised and updated edition). New York, NY: Oxford University Press.

McAdams, D. P., & de St. Aubin, E. (1992). A theory of generativity and its assessment through self-report, behavioral acts, and narrative themes in autobiography. *Journal of Personality and Social Psychology, 62*, 1003–1015.

McAdams, D. P., Diamond, A., de St. Aubin, E., & Mansfield, E. D. (1997). Stories of commitment: The psychosocial construction of generative lives. *Journal of Personality and Social Psychology, 72*, 678–694.

McAdams, D. P., Josselson, R., & Lieblich, A. (Eds.). (2006). *Identity and story: Creating self in narrative.* Washington, DC: APA Books.

McAdams, D. P., & McLean, K. C. (2013). Narrative identity. *Current Directions in Psychological Science, 22*, 233–238.

McAdams, D. P., & Olson, B. (2010). Personality development: Continuity and change over the life course. In S. T. Fiske, D. L. Schacter, & R. Sternberg (Eds.), *Annual review of psychology* (Vol. 61, pp. 517–542). Palo Alto, CA: Annual Reviews.

McAdams, D. P., Reynolds, J., Lewis, M., Patten, A., & Bowman, P. J. (2001). When bad things turn good and good things turn bad: Sequences of redemption and contamination in life narrative, and their relation to psychosocial adaptation in midlife adults and in students. *Personality and Social Psychology Bulletin, 27*, 472–483.

McLean, K. C., Pasupathi, M., & Pals, J. L. (2007). Selves creating stories creating selves: A process model of self-development. *Personality and Social Psychology Review, 11*, 262–278.

Mischel, W. (1968). *Personality and assessment.* New York, NY: Wiley.

Mischel, W. (2004). Toward an integrative science of the person. In S. T. Fiske, D. L. Schacter, & C. Zahn-Waxler (Eds.), *Annual review of psychology* (Vol. 55, pp. 1–22). Palo Alto, CA: Annual Reviews.

Mroczek, D. K., & Little, T. D. (Eds.). (2006). *Handbook of personality development.* Mahwah, NJ: Erlbaum.

Pasupathi, M., & Mansour, E. (2006). Adult age differences in autobiographical reasoning in narratives. *Developmental Psychology, 42*, 798–808.

Polkinghorne, D. (1988). *Narrative knowing and the human sciences.* Albany, NY: SUNY Press.

Roberts, B. W., Kuncel, N. R., Shiner, R. L., Caspi, A., & Goldberg, L. R. (2007). The power of personality: The comparative validity of personality traits, socio-economic status, and cognitive ability for predicting important life outcomes. *Perspectives on Psychological Science, 2*, 313–345.

Rosenwald, G. C., & Ochberg, R. L. (Eds.). (1992). *Storied lives: The cultural politics of self-understanding.* New Haven, CT: Yale University Press.

Rossi, A. (Ed.). (2001). *Caring and doing for others.* Chicago, IL: University of Chicago Press.

Sarbin, T. (Ed.). (1986). *Narrative psychology: The storied nature of human conduct.* New York, NY: Praeger.

Shotter, J., & Gergen, K. J. (Eds.). (1989). *Texts of identity.* London, UK: Sage.

Singer, J. A. (2004). Narrative identity and meaning-making across the adult lifespan: An introduction. *Journal of Personality, 72*, 437–459.

Stern, W. (1938). *General psychology: From the personalistic standpoint.* New York, NY: Macmillan.

Walker, L., & Frimer, J. (2007). Moral personality of brave and caring exemplars. *Journal of Personality and Social Psychology, 93,* 845–860.

DAN P. MCADAMS *is a professor of psychology at Northwestern University in Evanston, Illinois.*

NEW DIRECTIONS FOR CHILD AND ADOLESCENT DEVELOPMENT • DOI: 10.1002/cad

Lieblich, A. (2014). Narrating your life after 65 (or: To tell or not to tell, that is the question). In B. Schiff (Ed.), *Rereading Personal Narrative and Life Course. New Directions for Child and Adolescent Development, 145*, 71–83.

# 6

# Narrating Your Life After 65 (or: To Tell or Not to Tell, That Is the Question)

*Amia Lieblich*

## Abstract

*This chapter examines differential circumstances whereby aging individuals construct their selves as a narrative or, alternatively, seem to prefer other routes to manifest their identity. The preliminary exploration of questions about the characteristics of those aged who prefer to tell and those who do not, as well as the salutary role of telling, is based on two studies of 65–80-year-old well-functioning Israeli-Jewish seniors. While approximately half of them were willing to conduct a life review, the other half constructed their robust identity through activities and a here-and-now focus. Historical circumstances that involve seeing one's life story as heroic or having an important historical message, as opposed to a series of haphazard events, are considered a major factor in the preference to tell or not to tell. The chapter concludes that there are different strategies for identity management, with an emphasis on either past events or present activities. Neither of these preferences can simply indicate success or failure in aging well. © 2014 Wiley Periodicals, Inc.*

New Directions for Child and Adolescent Development, no. 145, Fall 2014 © 2014 Wiley Periodicals, Inc.
Published online in Wiley Online Library (wileyonlinelibrary.com). • DOI: 10.1002/cad.20068

## Introduction

While recent scholarship, as documented in this volume, indicates that development may be conceptualized as an interpretative, narrative project, the present chapter examines differential circumstances whereby aging individuals do construct their selves as a narrative or, alternatively, seem to prefer other routes to manifest their identity. This issue, namely the manner in which seniors tell, or choose not to tell, their life stories, can be seen as a dialogue with two classical theoretical works: Cohler's (1982) pioneering work on *Personal Narrative and Life Course* and Butler's (1963/1968) article *The Life Review: An Interpretation of Reminiscence in the Aged*—both are seminal works for our understanding of narratives and aging. A more recent paper by Cohler (1993), *Aging, Morale, and Meaning: The Nexus of Narrative*, sheds additional light on the subject.

Within this theoretical context, on the empirical side, I would like to briefly present my relevant findings of two narrative studies conducted in Israel. In these studies, I encountered two opposite inclinations among aged men and women, who I asked to share their life story with me; while some tended to agree to tell their stories, others chose not to agree, yet both types of responses were colored with similar emotional intensity and persistence. In other words, the agreement was given with enthusiasm and the refusal was expressed with finality. Generally, the group of those who agreed to tell their life story was slightly larger. However, the proportion of persons who agreed or disagreed differed greatly between the two studies. This chapter will focus on and explore this interesting polarity.

Some clarifications need to be made first. There is a proliferation of terms used in psychology for the act of recounting one's life and they do not carry identical connotations (Haber, 2006). The three terms most relevant to the literature dealing with aging and stories, and to my own studies, are reminiscence, life review, and life story or narrative. All three are based on memory, in itself an important and intricate function when related to aging. Although scholars may use these terms indistinguishably, I believe that there is clear distinction between them. *Reminiscence*, which occurs spontaneously, relates to the act of bringing up memories, often fragments such as isolated episodes, and thus is entirely focused on the past. *Life review* is an active and intentional process, it is comprehensive, and emphasizes balancing the positive and the negative (e.g., success vs. failure) in one's lifetime. Although it may be repeated several times during one's lifetime, a life review is often a distinct project that one carries out. It often includes a future perspective, as in a decision to change, repent, etc. Scholars and lay people tend to agree that reminiscence and life review are especially prevalent among the aged. However, some empirical work refutes this claim (e.g., Webster, 1994). The third term, *life story* or *life narrative*, is a concept stressing the dynamic, on-going process of constructing our lives as a coherent story, which is also our identity (McAdams, 1993; Randall, 2001).

NEW DIRECTIONS FOR CHILD AND ADOLESCENT DEVELOPMENT • DOI: 10.1002/cad

The present moment is a major component in a life story. It is context-related and changing, but common at all ages after puberty (Habermas & Bluck, 2000). This third term is the one I have utilized most in my own academic work, and in that I share Cohler's preference. As concluded by Haber (2006), some of the disagreement in the field regarding the place and value of life stories among the aged results from the imprecise usage of the three terms mentioned above.

Another basic clarification concerns the definition of "old age." Different demarcations of "old age" have been proposed in different historical times, cultures, and societies. Definitions also vary depending on their purpose. With the recent prolongation of life expectancy in the West, "old age" has become a very long period in the life span. For Erikson, who wrote in the middle of the 20th century, "old age" started at 60. Today, however, 60 is considered the end of "midlife." For many, "old age" lasts for two or three decades after this boundary, with plenty of physical, psychological, and social changes taking place. As proposed by Neugarten (1996), in order to reach agreement in research and theory about the elderly, our claims should distinguish among the young–old (65–75), the old–old (75–85), and the oldest of the old (85 and beyond).

In my research, conducted in Israel during the last decade, I studied mostly the young–old group. I used the age of 65 as the minimal boundary for my participants because this is normally the age of retirement. Although my work is most relevant to the young–old, most of the research and theory in gerontology, including Butler (1963/1968), is predominantly about old–old women and men. The old people investigated in many of these classical studies, and at the focus of the theories proposed about aging, were seldom still living independently. Mostly, they lived in institutions and often suffered from depression. In all these respects they are very different from my participants, who are mostly retired but still active and independent 65–80-year-old citizens. Findings concerning this subgroup cannot be simply generalized to the "old–old" groups and vice versa.

## Cohler and Butler—Pioneering Ideas

In his 1982 chapter *Personal Narrative and Life Course,* Cohler suggested that human development is an ongoing process of life story formations by which individuals make sense of their lives and the world around them. The self, he was perhaps the first to claim, is a narrative, creative, ongoing project of constructing a cohesive account of one's past and present, in the context of one's culture and time. "People attempt successive subjective reformulations of their own life history across the course of life," he said (p. 207). As Schiff (Chapter 1 of this volume) emphasized, the project of rewriting our life story surfaces particularly during periods of transition or adversity. For Cohler, the transition into old age, with the discontinuity it often introduces into life, is often such a period. The rising awareness

of mortality leads individuals to become more concerned with their past
and involved in reorganizing their personal life experiences into meaningful
narratives. In a later chapter, Cohler succinctly stated that "a sense of psychological well-being in later life is assumed to be associated with enhanced
preservation of meaning, expressed as a purposive or coherent life story"
(Cohler, 1993, p. 108). This is also how Cohler considered the wisdom that
is attributed to the aged.

Butler's (1963/1968) work in the 1960s has been no less groundbreak-
ing. Fifty years later, it is evident that this early writing changed the stereo-
type of old people in general, and particularly their tendency to talk a lot
about their past, namely to reminiscence. As formulated by Haber (2006)
40 years later, "he began to remove the stigma associated with reminiscence and life review among older adults" (p. 155). Thus, behavior which
had been considered pathological, repetitive ruminations signifying with-
drawal from the present reality, was suddenly conceived as life review, a useful and healthy activity, manifesting "candor, serenity and wisdom" (Butler,
1963/1968, p. 486). Butler's seminal contribution resulted in numerous ap-
plications, introducing life review procedures (e.g., Haight, 1988; Haight &
Olson, 1989) into the elderly's institutionalized and private care. Moreover,
for me, Butler's work marks the onset of the movement of "positive aging"
(Gergen & Gergen, 2010; Lieblich, 2014), a movement to which Cohler's
work also contributed a great deal.

Thus, we may ask the following questions: Do old people construct
their selves via narratives, and do these narratives have age-specific characteristics? In what way are historical-cultural factors involved in their narratives or explain their narrative absence? More specifically: Are the elderly
indeed particularly prone to tell about their past lives as compared to other
age groups? How is the inclination to narrate manifested? What may characterize the aged who prefer to tell, or rather not to tell? Is telling beneficial
for one's well-being? A preliminary exploration of these questions is offered
by the described studies, which look at spontaneous or intentional life story
narrating in the lives of young–old independent men and women in Israel
at the onset of the 21st century.

## Description of My Studies

In Study 1 (Lieblich, 2007a), a narrative study, I conducted life story interviews with a group of 51 individuals aged 65–72, all of them child survivors
of a battle that took place in Israel during the 1948 War of Independence.
During this war, they all lost their homes in Kibbutz Kfar Etzion, and 47 of
them lost their fathers.[1] The purpose of the study, initiated by two of the
group members, was to write a book about them, thus to make their collective story known to the public, a part of history. My opening question
for the in-depth interview, which lasted between 90 minutes and 4 hours,
was "Please tell me about your life from childhood onwards, starting with
the stories you heard about your father and the Kibbutz where you were

NEW DIRECTIONS FOR CHILD AND ADOLESCENT DEVELOPMENT • DOI: 10.1002/cad

born." The reading, interpretation, and analysis of the extensive narrative data I collected focused mainly on two different topics—coping with loss and growing up as an orphan (Lieblich, 2008a), and the construction of collective memory (Lieblich, 2007b).

In Study 2 (Lieblich, 2008b, 2014), I initiated a combined narrative and participant observation research project in a particular beach community near my home. During my early morning walks with my dog, I noticed some elderly people who regularly walked along the same seashore. Many of them individually practiced exercise routines and then gathered daily in a beach café for some games and morning drinks. I became interested in these people and adopted the habit of drinking coffee at the café. I started to keep a field journal about the people and after a while I proposed to interview the regulars and write about them. The opening question was "Please tell me your life story. When did you start coming daily to this beach and why?" Life story interviews were successfully carried out with 30 members of the beach community. They were shorter than the ones conducted in my first study and most of them took place at the café, which was not an entirely private setting. In addition, I recorded many conversations that took place among the members and with me.

The data collection for these two studies was accomplished more or less in parallel. The participants in these two studies were of similar ages, 65–80 years old, with a majority around 70, and they were all Israeli Jews. However, in other respects, they differed a great deal. Compared to the strong ties of shared history which bind the members of the first group, the second community was relatively sporadic and transient. Members of the first group were mostly orthodox, religious Jews, and had obtained higher education and relatively high SES positions in Israel. Members of the second study were secular, had only elementary education, and mostly belonged to the lower middle class. While interviewees from the first group were all Israeli-born, all members of the second group were immigrants. Finally, as mentioned above, the beach community study was an outcome of my own enterprise, while the Kibbutz survivors' study was a product of their own initiative.

It is impossible to summarize the findings or the narratives of these two projects here. The present chapter will focus only on the role of telling one's life story, giving a life review, or exhibiting reminiscence—as manifested in the behavior of the elderly participants of the two studies.

**Study 1.** In my initial contact with the second generation of Kibbutz Kfar Etzion founders, I easily obtained their consent to be interviewed and scheduled private meetings to listen to their stories. Since this group is well defined, and moreover they—and their families—meet regularly at least once a year, at the common memorial services for their deceased fathers, I had a clear perspective on the group's boundaries and a complete and up-to-date mailing list of the membership. In 2003–2004, when I started my interviews, 56 women and men belonged to the child survivors' group.

Fifty-one consent letters were promptly returned, including two from persons living outside of Israel at the time. This proportion of consent is itself a significant finding. (I was prepared to carry out the research if only 50% of the membership agreed to participate!)

Not only did they agree, but their willingness was also manifested in the ease and flexibility of setting a time and place for our meetings. All these people shared with me detailed, sensitive, and profound life stories. In spite of the fact that the conversations were often sad, and painful memories came up, all of them expressed deep gratitude for providing them with the opportunity to recount their life and family history. This response grew when the book was published and well accepted by the Israeli public.[2]

Basically, individuals of this sample provided an impressive and highly cohesive life story, which confirms Cohler's theory about the importance of coherent life stories for our well-being and coping with challenges and transitions. Their stories focused on the meaning (historical or religious) of their early suffering and their fathers' death. Almost none of these individuals, who were then about 65–70 years old, complained about the difficulties of aging. They considered themselves in their prime, yet very proud of their adult children and grandchildren.

As I gradually learned in the project, the members of this survivors' group decided, individually and collectively, to complete a life review. Their high motivation to narrate their life story was an outcome of several components: First and foremost, the narrators saw the study as a way to commemorate their deceased parents and pay tribute to the battle of Kfar Etzion in 1948. A great part of the stories delivered in this study told about their fathers who were killed, the battle in which their demise took place, and the village that was destroyed. In telling their stories, these individuals wanted to rescue their dear ones from oblivion. This is an expression of the common human need to be heard and remembered as part of the history of one's society or community—a motive that resonates also with the concept of generativity proposed by Erikson (1950) and studied further by McAdams and de St. Aubin (1998). By telling me their personal narratives, the child survivors were constructing the collective memory of their group, as a chapter in the collective memory of Israel. This motivational trend is clearly embedded in the narrators' sense of belonging to a community and their loyalty to their society, whose history concerns them. Moreover, in talking to me as a writer, who will make their story public, I often felt that I had become an instrument for their mission or generativity, particularly that they were talking to their children and grandchildren, and to the next generation in general, through the printed chapters of the book.

Another motivation was to "prove" that their lives had not been damaged by their childhood losses and traumas. Nevertheless, they often saw the opportunity to tell their story to a patient and respectful other as providing ventilation for pent-up pain and an occasion to mourn. Several interviews were interrupted by crying. And yet, the major message was: "Look at me, in spite of all this, I have become a healthy, happy and productive person." In support of Butler's thesis, this group clearly exhibited the need to evaluate and review one's life. They undertook this mission before they might be too old or feeble for it. This is obviously easier to do when the balance of one's life narrative tends toward the positive. But, of course, do we not all construct our life stories to convey a favorable balance? I believe so, but it is not always possible, as we will see.

A few quotations from the book demonstrate the claims made above:[3]

Esther (65): "Always, as a child, and even in the army, I felt different from others. I always felt as if I belong to something else, to another place. My mother remarried but I have never felt completely part of that new family. I felt that I belonged to another family, with a father that I hardly remember. All the people, who knew me, knew that there was another part to my life, an important and unique part of my history that I share with others. I was always the special girl on memorial days… This was typical of me—longing for something, for another world, that I cannot reach because it is lost forever." (Lieblich, 2007a, p. 442)

Israel (65): "The fact that I come from Kfar Etzion and that my father was killed there effects my whole approach to my life in this country. I have understood that one has to pay a price for living here, it doesn't come for free. There is a profound connection between our sacrifice and the existence of the state of Israel." (Lieblich, 2007a, p. 455)

Hanan (68): "Do understand, as I repeat so many times: what we felt, as the children of Kfar Etzion, a tiny group, for this piece of land which we had to give up, is—if you multiply by a hundred thousand—what the entire Jewish people felt throughout history for the land of our nation. The entire Jewish history of loss, exile, redemption and rebirth is contained in our little history in a nutshell." (Lieblich, 2007a, p. 394)

**Study 2.** In contrast to the Kfar Etzion study, when I approached the members of the beach community, I often encountered a refusal to share one's life story. Since this was a much more informal project, I did not record all my failed attempts, but I estimate that only about half, or less, of the people who I approached consented to be interviewed. Moreover, I had no alternative but to conduct the interviews in the café on the beach, during regular daily visits, without sufficient privacy and quiet; almost none of the people I invited to participate were willing to set aside a special time and place for the conversation. It required repeated attempts to procure the 30 interviews that I finally carried out. In other words, the motivation of the seaside community members to talk about the past was much lower.

As I attended the field daily, even when no interview was scheduled, I had the opportunity to listen to the regular clients' spontaneous conversations. One of my strongest conclusions in the study was that the discourse on the beach was predominantly a "here-and-now" affair, where the weather, the conditions of the sea and sand, the fish, or the young women who passed by were the topics of preference. Although, on average, the age of the regular clients was 70 or more, they absolutely did not tend to reminiscence in public.

The orientation toward the present moment was the essence of many of the refusals I encountered, such as: "Why tell about my life, there is nothing to tell"; "Please don't ruin my morning"; "The present day is so beautiful, who wants to dwell on past memories?"; "The past is gone. We are here and that is all that matters." This frequently expressed attitude toward the past supports Cohler's (1993) claim that "older adults live much more in the present than do younger adults" (p. 120). As I got to know the people of this seaside group better, I understood that for many of them the past cannot be seen as a source of solace or of pride. Their previous hardships cannot be vested with meanings, and, thus, their decision to leave it behind is healthy. In contradiction to Butler (1963/1968) and Erikson (1978), these people's memory or life story cannot provide a foundation for the maintenance of their morale in later life.

An additional factor, which may or may not be the outcome of a lack of pride in their past, is that the beach community, and especially the men, have developed an admiration for silence. They dedicate their time and energy to *doing* (sports and games, for example) rather than storytelling. The wise man exercises, jokes, drinks, or plays games in company—with little verbal output. In general, compared to the men, the women from this seaside community were more ready and sometimes even keen to present their life story, but among women, too, refusals were very frequent.

Thus, the essential difference that emerged between the two studies was that the first group willingly undertook the process of life review because they were able to conceive of their past as serving their values and ideals, or highly meaningful as a historical lesson, while the second group did not share this tendency because they had a hard time finding pride and meaning in their past. Moreover, I believe that this group, consisting mostly of immigrants, might have experienced a form of survivors' guilt. This has much to do with the prevalent attitudes and prejudices of Israelis toward new immigrants who came after the establishment of the State of Israel, whether Holocaust survivors (Kangisser-Cohen, 2005) or refugees from Muslim countries. The members of the beach community who did consent to be interviewed were the ones who managed to construct their stories as a heroic struggle against adverse life conditions. Yet even they hailed the present moment while being interviewed about their past!

The following is a summary of a dialogue that demonstrates the preference to abstain from telling.[4] I was trying to interview Simon, 80, one of the oldest members of the beach community. After many attempts and much pleading on my behalf, he finally sat with me in the corner of the café and started by telling me that he emigrated from Germany to Palestine in 1935 and had been coming to our beach every morning for 40 years.

"And do you have any memories from that early time on the beach?" I asked.

"Memories! What memories! Why should I try to recall the past? I can't remember what happened yesterday! Anyway, what happened since 1935 is a long, long story. We don't have the time for it."

It was clear that Simon was looking for excuses to avoid talking about his past. When I insisted, he provided a superficial chronology about his business achievements and geographical moves. Of all of his early memories, he only dwelt on being wounded, a fact that couldn't be concealed. Throughout his monologue, he made various disparaging comments, like "all this is nonsense." About 15 minutes into our conversation, he mentioned his children in passing.

"But you didn't tell me about getting married," I protested.

My protest seemed to upset Simon's fragile consent to provide a life story. He got up from his seat, said that he had some business elsewhere and ended our conversation.

"OK, tomorrow you will tell me about your family and your love for the sea," I said.

"I don't think so! I've blabbered enough. I have never told anyone any of these old tales, and enough is enough!"

In comparison, it is interesting to analyze the contents of the consenting subgroup of participants. As mentioned above, consent was mostly given by women, who provided impressive, wise, and content-filled narratives. Three women stood out in their life review—a Holocaust survivor, an immigrant from Egypt, and a woman who grew up in extreme poverty in Tel Aviv. All three had overcome difficult circumstances and constructed coherent life stories as a heroic climb toward better life, gaining insights that they wanted to share about values, priorities, family life, and other universal matters.[5]

## Discussion

While generalizations from these case studies should be made with caution, the following section refers to the questions posed in my introduction and lays the ground for future inquiry and exposition.

First and foremost, my studies on the life stories of two groups of high functioning "young–old" Israelis show that not all of them are willing to conduct a life review at this stage nor do they indulge in spontaneous reminiscence. This replicates findings of both quantitative and qualitative work that came to similar conclusions (Wink & Schiff, 2002). As Wink and Schiff (2002) argue, most people may never review their lives—they simply do not have the need to do so or are too busy and active at this stage. Furthermore,

NEW DIRECTIONS FOR CHILD AND ADOLESCENT DEVELOPMENT • DOI: 10.1002/cad

there is no evidence in my study that the ones who do review their lives are better adjusted.

These findings give rise to several speculations, some of which are profoundly related to Cohler's contributions about narratives and aging and concern the narrative nature of identity (Freeman, Chapter 7 of this volume). Let me first discuss the two types of responses separately: those who provided a life story upon my invitation and those who did not.

The seniors who were willing to be interviewed constructed their identity through their narratives and were ready to convey it as their life story. Whether part of the majority of the Kfar Etzion group or the minority of the seaside community, all these narrators were able to look back on their life with pride and satisfaction. They were aware of their generativity in telling a historical or personal tale of value and worth, a narrative that can be conceived as a lesson to future generations (McAdams, Chapter 5 of this volume). The offspring of Kfar Etzion adopted an identity that included a historical mission, namely an obligation to construct or preserve the collective memory of their community. Their narratives had high relevance to the collective narrative of the redemption of the Jewish people in the 20th century and their individual or family role within this "big story" (Bamberg, 2006). This confirms Cohler's claim that narratives are always told in social-historical time, and as such may be evaluated in terms of their contribution to some higher ethos of their period and culture. For the Kfar Etzion offspring, their "big story" was that of Jewish fate and Israeli heroism. Similarly, for the minority of the seaside community members who did construct their lives as narratives, their "big story" may be that of mastering difficulties through individual agency, for example, overcoming the immense hardships of the Holocaust or of immigration and poverty.

In comparison, the group of individuals who did not provide a life review or dwell on reminiscence constructed their robust identity through activities and a here-and-now focus. These men and women were very modest and saw themselves as minute elements in the upheavals of the world. In general, they were unable to construct their narratives as either heroic or having an important historical message, but more as a series of haphazard events—"small stories" (Bamberg, 2006) that had happened to them. Considering these observations, I think that because aging involves a certain amount of decline for almost everyone, elders may suppress unhappy narratives, unless they carry an important message of some sort. They may have a private version of a life story, as we all do, but they are not as keen to share it in public, particularly with a stranger. Furthermore, perhaps they are trying to protect their intimate story from being transformed by the stranger's eye or the mere experience of telling.

The above argument is further related to the fact that the two groups were different in their religiosity. For people of faith, such as the Kfar Etzion offspring, the idea that "this is God's will, which I may be unable to fathom" provides a framework for a coherent story, even for a turbulent life.

When such a religious framework of meaning is missing, one's story may be experienced as shameful, manifesting weakness or lacking coherence, and therefore silenced.

Thus, these two studies indicate that, for the elderly, narrating one's life is not universally the means for establishing a firm and hopeful identity. Although my participants were old, they were mostly young–old, to adopt Neugarten's distinction. They were still able to enjoy active, joyful social and physical life, activities that provided the basis for their identity. Without a historical, religious, or ideological message to society, the inclination to conduct a life review seemed to be less pressing than previously suggested by the literature.

Narrating one's life story is not an essential component of successful aging for all, or equally for all stages of aging. However, it does provide solace to some of the elderly, and perhaps particularly so for the oldest of the old. Research about who is inclined to tell their life story, and when or how telling one's life story is beneficial, is not conclusive yet, but practices of "narrative gerontology" (e.g., Haight, 1988; Kenyon, Bohlmeijer, & Randall, 2011; Kenyon, Clark, & de Vries, 2001) have been widely utilized for the last three decades and, according to the practitioners who employ them, have much to offer to the well-being of the aged.

To conclude, there are different strategies for identity management and engagement with the past is just one. Old people may construct their identity by telling stories about the past or by other, more physical, active means that focus on the present. Neither of these preferences can simply indicate success or failure in aging well. Indeed, there might be no rules to narrative and aging. As Neugarten argues, the older we become, the more different we become.

## References

Bamberg, M. (2006). Stories: Big or small? Why do we care? In M. Bamberg (Ed.), Narrative—State of the art (pp. 165–174). Amsterdam, The Netherlands: John Benjamins.

Butler, R. N. (1963/1968). The life review: An interpretation of reminiscence in the aged. In B. L. Neugarten (Ed.), Middle age and aging: A reader in social psychology (pp. 486–496). Chicago, IL: The University of Chicago Press.

Cohler, B. J. (1982). Personal narrative and life course. In P. Baltes & O. G. Brim (Eds.), Life span development and behavior (Vol. 4, pp. 205–241). New York, NY: Academic Press.

Cohler, B. J. (1993). Aging, morale, and meaning: The nexus of narrative. In T. Cole, W. Achenbaum, P. Jakobi, & R. Kastenbaum (Eds.), Voices and visions of aging: Toward a critical gerontology (pp. 107–133). New York, NY: Springer.

Erikson, E. H. (1950). Childhood and society. New York, NY: Norton.

Erikson, E. H. (1978). Reflections on Dr. Borg's life cycle. In E. H. Erikson (Ed.), Adulthood (pp. 1–32). New York, NY: Norton.

Gergen, K. J., & Gergen, M. (2010). Positive aging: Resilience and reconstruction. In P. S. Fry & C. L. M. Keyes (Eds.), New frontiers in resilient aging: Life strengths and wellness in later life (pp. 340–356). Cambridge, UK: Cambridge University Press.

Haber, D. (2006). Life review: Implementation, theory, research and therapy. *International Journal of Aging and Human Development, 63*(2), 153–171.

Habermas, T., & Bluck, S. (2000). Getting a life: The emergence of the life story in adolescence. *Psychological Bulletin, 126,* 748–769.

Haight, B. (1988). The therapeutic role of a structured life review process in homebound elderly subjects. *Journal of Gerontology, 43*(2), 40–44.

Haight, B., & Olson, M. (1989). Teaching home health aides the use of life review. *Journal of Nursing Staff Development, 5,* 11–16.

Herzog, C., & Gazit, S. (1982/2005). *The Arab-Israeli wars: War and peace in the Middle East.* New York, NY: Vintage Books.

Kangisser-Cohen, S. (2005). *Child survivors of the Holocaust in Israel.* Brighton, UK: Sussex Academic Press.

Kenyon, G., Bohlmeijer, E., & Randall, W. L. (Eds.). (2011). *Storying later life: Issues, investigations and interventions in narrative gerontology.* New York, NY: Oxford University Press.

Kenyon, G., Clark, P., & de Vries, B. (Eds.). (2001). *Narrative gerontology: Theory, research and practice.* New York, NY: Springer.

Lieblich, A. (2007a). *The children of Kfar Etzion.* Haifa, Israel: University of Haifa Press (Hebrew).

Lieblich, A. (2007b). The second generation of Kfar Etzion: A study of collective memory. In D. Mendels (Ed.), *On memory, an interdisciplinary approach* (pp. 213–230). Oxford, UK: Peter Lang.

Lieblich, A. (2008a). The place of religion in the experience of war-orphans as constructed in their life stories. In J. A. Belzen & A. Geels (Eds.), *Autobiography and the psychological study of religious lives* (pp. 239–253). Amsterdam, The Netherlands: Rodopi.

Lieblich, A. (2008b). *Arak for breakfast.* Tel Aviv, Israel: Schocken (Hebrew).

Lieblich, A. (2014). *Narratives of positive aging: Seaside stories.* New York, NY: Oxford University Press.

McAdams, D. P. (1993). *The stories we live by.* New York, NY: Guilford Press.

McAdams, D. P., & de St. Aubin, E. (Eds.). (1998). *Generativity and adult development: How and why we care for the next generation.* Washington, DC: American Psychological Association.

Neugarten, B. L. (Ed.). (1996). *The meaning of age.* Chicago, IL: University of Chicago Press.

Randall, W. (2001). Storied worlds: Acquiring a narrative perspective on aging, identity and everyday life. In G. Kenyon, P. Clark, & B. Vries (Eds.), *Narrative gerontology* (pp. 31–61). New York, NY: Springer.

Webster, J. (1994). Predictors of reminiscence: A lifespan perspective. *Canadian Journal of Aging, 13,* 66–78.

Wink, P., & Schiff, B. (2002). To review or not to review? The role of personality and life events in life review and adaptation to older age. In J. D. Webster & B. K. Haight (Eds.), *Critical advances in reminiscence work: From theory to application* (pp. 44–60). New York, NY: Springer.

## Notes

1. For more information, see the battle of Kfar Etzion in Herzog and Gazit (1982/2005).

2. Of the small minority of group members who refused to be interviewed, three could be characterized as people undergoing severe difficulty at the time of the study (financial, marital, or mental crisis), one was engrossed in writing his own book about

his individual narrative and therefore refused to participate, and one simply drifted away and did not keep any contacts with this group.

3. These quotes are translated from Hebrew (Lieblich, 2007a).
4. This is an abridged adaptation from Lieblich (2014).
5. These narratives will appear in full in Lieblich (2014).

AMIA LIEBLICH *is professor emerita at The Hebrew University of Jerusalem and president of the Academic College for Society and the Arts in Israel.*

Freeman, M. (2014). "Personal Narrative and Life Course" revisited: Bert Cohler's legacy for developmental psychology. In B. Schiff (Ed.), *Rereading Personal Narrative and Life Course*. New Directions for Child and Adolescent Development, 145, 85–96.

7

# "Personal Narrative and Life Course" Revisited: Bert Cohler's Legacy for Developmental Psychology

*Mark Freeman*

## Abstract

*The primary aims of this concluding chapter are to identify common themes across the preceding chapters, to provide an integrative synthesis of these themes, and to draw out the implications of Bertram Cohler's work for narrative psychology and for the field of developmental psychology more generally. As with the previous chapters, the central ideas explored in* Personal Narrative and Life Course *remain focal to the discussion. So too is the concept of development, in childhood, adolescence, and beyond. By drawing together the retrospective dimension frequently associated with the idea of narrative with the prospective dimension frequently associated with the idea of development, this chapter also seeks to underscore Cohler's seminal contribution to our understanding of the dynamic movement of human lives in and through time. © 2014 Wiley Periodicals, Inc.*

NEW DIRECTIONS FOR CHILD AND ADOLESCENT DEVELOPMENT, no. 145, Fall 2014 © 2014 Wiley Periodicals, Inc.
Published online in Wiley Online Library (wileyonlinelibrary.com). • DOI: 10.1002/cad.20069

## Narrative and Development

I n the very first paragraph of *Personal Narrative and Life Course* (Cohler, 1982), we read that "Understanding the manner in which persons maintain a sense of coherence of self and consistency of the life history remains an important problem in the study of lives" (p. 206). Indeed it does, still. It has also become the target of some significant criticism, particularly by those who wish to cast into question the classic beginning-middle-end view of narrative, where everything fits together nicely and neatly. But this view was never Cohler's view, and, for the most part, it is not the view of those who continue to consider the idea of coherence important, including some of those (e.g., McAdams, Chapter 5 of this volume) found in the pages of this volume. Rather, the idea is that amid all the changes and accidents and twists and turns that come our way and that inevitably render our lives much more tortuous and unpredictable than the classic view would hold, there emerges a need—more acutely felt in some than others, to be sure—but a need nonetheless. And that need is to make sense of our lives, to extract some semblance of unity, of *identity*, out of difference. So, "The concept of the personal narrative as order which is imposed upon a developmental course inherently unpredictable is consistent with perspectives on personality emphasizing the importance *both* of order and of change across the course of life" (Cohler, 1982, p. 206; emphasis added).

I happen to differ with the way some of this is framed. From my perspective, narrative is not so much "imposed" on our lives as it is woven into its very fabric (Freeman, 1998, 2003). I also think that just as incoherence can be a problem, requiring the "intervention" of narrative, so too can coherence: we can sometimes become prisoners of our own stories, holding onto them for dear life, even in the face of their palpable destructiveness or falsity (Freeman, 2010a, 2010b). Nevertheless, the basic criterion being considered here—"narrative intelligibility," as Cohler refers to it, following Paul Ricoeur (1984)—remains paramount and does well to preserve the needed tension between continuity and change, identity and difference.

It is a short step from this first issue, concerning coherence and how it might be thought about, to the second, which is about the interpretive or "hermeneutic" dimension of narrative. "The traditional, explanatory approach," Cohler writes, "based on a nineteenth-century model of the natural sciences, was concerned primarily with demonstration of stability or ordered change in lives over time" (p. 209). In addition, we might add, it was rooted in a temporal and causal framework predicated upon the idea and ideal of predictability: the movement of lives followed the well-known arrow of time, moving inexorably forward, the "if" of event A leading, one hoped, to the "then" (or the "probably then") of event B. "In contrast to this explanatory approach," Cohler's argument continues, "the interpretive or narrative approach is based on an assumption that lives change over time in ways not necessarily predictable" (p. 210) and that, as such, we should recognize and indeed embrace the possibilities inherent in looking *back-ward* in time, in the manner of the historian, and seeing how, even amid such change, one can generally extract a thread, a through-line, that allows one to see life events as *episodes* in an evolving narrative (Freeman, 1984, 1991).

As Cohler recognized, there are of course problems with this move, not least because we have shifted from the realm of causally based explanation of the if/then sort to *interpretation*, on the part of both the people being studied and also the researcher doing the studying. This simple fact is unlikely to sit well with those who like their empirical psychology straight up, so to speak. But this hermeneutic dimension of narrative psychology—this *dual* hermeneutic, more specifically—is patently unsurpassable. The question, therefore, and the challenge, is how to generate viable knowledge given the irrevocably interpretive nature of the endeavor. It is not one easily solved, and it has resulted in all kinds of theoretical and philosophical contortions about validity, truth, and so on.

I believe some of Cohler's ideas in *Personal Narrative and Life Course* can help us work through some of these issues. Yes, the hermeneutic dimension is unsurpassable. Memory, for instance, Cohler points out, is rarely to be seen as some sort of photographic reproduction of the past–present but instead consists of "present reflections on earlier experiences, successively transformed across childhood and adulthood. . . . At any one point in the life course," therefore, "the personal narrative represents a particular interpretation, experienced as internally consistent, of currently experienced memories. Memories based on subsequent experiences," in turn, "lead to successive reorganizations of the developmental gestalt" (pp. 212–213). This is fairly standard narrative fare.

Where it becomes decidedly *less* standard is when Cohler goes on to address specific developmental shifts in which these successive reorganizations take place. Indeed, what Cohler suggests, or at least implies, is that the aforementioned dual hermeneutic, which we found to be central to narrative psychology, is also central to *developmental* psychology. In order to get a handle on this very complicated issue, he begins by noting that "time itself is experienced in different ways across the life course." This is significant in its own right, and knowing how it happens, or tends to happen, can give us important clues about how personal narratives are constructed and what functions they might serve. This territory needs to be entered cautiously. Saying that children navigate time this way, that adolescents do it that way, and so on down the line can lead to a reified sense of the developmental process—which is to say, a view of the developmental process that Cohler seeks to move beyond. Nevertheless, his theoretical project in this piece—which is essentially to gain some sort of systematic developmental handle on the reconstructive process as it takes place throughout the life course—is a truly valiant one. It is not enough, he implies, to proclaim the inevitability of narrative reconstruction. The task, and the challenge, is

NEW DIRECTIONS FOR CHILD AND ADOLESCENT DEVELOPMENT • DOI: 10.1002/cad

instead to specify how it happens, and how it happens *differently*, at different phases of the life course.

Cohler's distinctive hermeneutic thus seeks to unite in some meaningful way the historical, or historiographical, and the developmental. "From this perspective," he explains, "the course of life may be better understood as a series of transformations representing marked discontinuities in development, rather than as transformations in which later phases appear to emerge from earlier ones." At the same time, he goes on to suggest, "The timing of these transformations is a consequence of intrinsic developmental processes, including maturation and related socially determined understandings of place in the life course, as well as particular life events and larger historical events. These transformations," he adds, "are characteristically dramatic and require considerable self-interpretive activity in order to preserve a sense of continuity in the personal narrative" (pp. 214–215). Not surprisingly, "It is at these times of transformation across the life course that feelings of fragmentation or personal integration are most likely to occur if such coherence cannot be maintained . . . explaining, for instance, the frequent appearance of the symptoms of schizophrenia first with attainment of adolescence" (p. 215).

Again, caution is warranted here. On the one hand, Cohler is highlighting developmental discontinuities. On the other hand, however, he is willing to refer to "intrinsic developmental processes," his apparent assumption being that there may in fact be a way to systematically frame the very continuities at hand. In all honesty, I have no idea how far to go with this—mainly because very few others have taken up the sort of challenge being posed. But I have often found this particular angle on narrative psychology to be a very provocative one, not least because it points in the direction of a rapprochement not only between continuity and change, and not only between development and history, but also between science and art. I shall say more about this in a short while.

## Developmental Transformations in the Personal Narrative

Cohler goes on to address three distinct transformations in the personal narrative: the "five-to-seven" shift, the transformation of adolescence and young (one might say "emerging") adulthood, and the shift from adulthood to middle age. For present purposes, there is no need to go into detail about these transformations. What does seem worth emphasizing is their dynamic, "motivated" nature. "With childhood amnesia," for instance, brought on by the Oedipal drama, "the remembered past becomes quite different from the past previously recalled" (p. 216). What Cohler also suggests in this context, drawing especially on Freud's (alleged) abandonment of the seduction hypothesis and his recognition of the primacy of psychic reality, is that "This focus upon a developmentally shaped fantasy world, rather than the time/space world, differentiates psychoanalytic accounts from all other accounts of human development" (p. 217). It also helps to underscore the primacy of *meaning* and, in turn, narrative. Cohler quotes an important passage from Freud (1910/1960) in this context: "Quite unlike conscious memories from the time of maturity, [childhood memories] are not fixed at the moment of being experienced, but are only elicited at a later age when childhood is already past; in the process, they are altered and falsified, and are put in the service of later trends, so that generally speaking, they cannot be sharply distinguished from fantasies" (p. 83).

I would like to add two qualifications here, and I think they are important ones. First, on my reading, Freud never completely abandoned the seduction hypothesis; all he did was supplement it with his emerging understanding that psychical reality could be every bit as developmentally formative—and deformative—as material reality. Nor did he abandon the idea of arriving at some essential truth of the life story. As important as psychical reality was and is, there still remained the challenge of fashioning something akin to a true account of the past. Second, the process of reconstruction is not only about memories being "altered and falsified," but also about what can be seen, with the passage of time, that could not be seen earlier on (Freeman, 2010a). Freud's (1895/1966) idea of *Nachtraglichkeit*—deferred action—is very much about this idea, and what it suggests is that memory and narrative can be vehicles of revelation as well as falsification. What it also suggests is that the developmental process cannot be bound by the aforementioned if/then version causation. Nor can it be bound by a framework that relies exclusively on linear time. For some of what happens during the course of time—a seduction, for instance, taking place in the earliest years of childhood—may not be identified as such until some subsequent point in time, at which point the event might *become* traumatic. Important though that the past "in itself" may be in certain instances, therefore, also important, Freud learned, is what one *makes* of the past through the ever-changing lens of the present. And this in turn suggests, once more, that the interpretive or hermeneutic dimension—specifically, the dimension of looking backward and discerning anew the meaning and significance of what has come before—is a key feature of the developmental process.

Following Miller, Chen, and Olivarez (Chapter 2 of this volume), the basic process being considered emerges earlier in development than has often been assumed. Indeed, they note, "By roughly two years of age children are able to participate in telling stories of their own past experiences in interaction with family members" (p. 18). Generally speaking, such stories are "simple, invoking departures from the baseline of their ordinary, expectable experience. These perturbations have emotional and moral import to the child and his significant others." Already, therefore, "only a few years into the life course, self making is demonstrably a narrative project" (p. 18). Alongside self making, Miller et al. go on to suggest, is self *re*-making. In accordance with Cohler's notion that "the project of constructing a personal narrative is never finished" and that "individuals narrate their lives time and time again," they underscore the fact that children, among others, "successively revisit and reformulate their interpretations, seeking to make sense of their lives in the face of change, both anticipated discontinuities and unanticipated contingencies" (p. 21). Along these lines, they assert that "Cohler's understanding of the dynamics of the personal narrative *in* time is his most profound and original insight" (p. 21) and that "the dynamic nature of narrative as an everyday practice is one of the strongest threads of continuity between the personal narrative and early development" (p. 22). Whether this understanding is Cohler's most profound and original insight is debatable, there are surely other contenders as well. One way or the other, "young children's immersion in personal storytelling helps to explain how this practice infiltrates their hearts and minds, becoming a means by which they render themselves intelligible to themselves and others" (p. 22). It also helps to explain why the process of development itself is a reconstructive project, wherein, via interpreting and reinterpreting the vicissitudes of one's past experience, one moves forward into the future.

Returning to the larger point Cohler is after in this context, the reconstructive process is notable not only for the well-known fact, following Bartlett (1932/1995) and others, that the past is always remembered and told from some present and is thus never to be seen in purely reproductive terms, but also for the fact that it is *motivated* by present needs and wishes and, especially, developmental demands (Ross, 1991; Ross & Wilson, 2000). An important challenge, therefore, again, is to begin to discern the specific nature of this motivation at different phases of development and, in turn, the changing meaning and function of the reconstructive process. This is important terrain, very much under thought. *Personal Narrative and Life Course* was critical in bringing it to light.

Cohler's comments on the second large developmental transformation, in adolescence, seem particularly important. It is at this phase, Cohler writes, drawing still on Freud, that "persons 'remodel' their histories in a manner analogous to that in which a nation much later rewrites its history in order to create successive legends about the past relevant to that later point in history" (Cohler, 1982, p. 218). But Erikson is the key player here, the reconstructive process now serving as a vehicle for the integration of past, present, and future and the formation of identity. Much of the current work being done on narrative identity picks up on these earlier formulations. According to Habermas and Hatiboğlu (Chapter 3 of this volume), this process of reconstructive integration, and its tendency to move in the direction of narrative *coherence*, is a key feature of the development of the life story in adolescence. So too, they suggest, is the burgeoning inclusion of *context* in making and remaking the life story. Habermas and Hatiboğlu thus speak of the "social contextualization of life," such that one's narrative becomes embedded not only in a personal context, issuing from one's present circumstances, but also "in a family constellation, a family history, a socioeconomic and sociocultural situation, and a historical situation" (p. 33).

In this respect, the reconstructive process in adolescence becomes progressively more hermeneutically sensitive, more intimately attuned to the ways in which one's life story and one's life itself are constituted in and through *tradition* (Gadamer, 1975; Shils, 1981). In speaking of tradition, I speak here not of that which the "traditionalist" might wish to maintain, but the sociohistorical ground within which life historical meaning emerges. Cohler's work, once again, was vitally important in bringing these issues to light, and Habermas and Hatiboğlu have done well to extend his insights into current theorizing about adolescent development.

Hammack and Toolis's chapter (Chapter 4 of this volume) moves further into the life course, focusing especially on emerging adulthood. Rather than addressing the process of "personal narrative construction," however, they speak of narrative *engagement*, which, in their view, "better describes the dynamic, dialogic process through which reconstructive, interpretive activity occurs" (p. 45). In line with Habermas and Hatiboğlu's emphasis on contextualization, as well as Cohler's own "sociogenic" perspective on the developmental process, Hammack and Toolis suggest that "adulthood represents a cultural discourse always associated with historical time and place," that "contemporary discourse on adulthood in the 21st century in much of the world is linked to the larger social and economic context of late capitalism," and, perhaps most importantly, that "the meaning of adulthood has shifted considerably" (p. 45) since 1982, when Cohler penned his essay. For them, therefore, "adulthood itself ought . . . to be conceived not as an inevitable moment of biological maturation but rather as a social and cultural discourse to which individuals orient their personal narratives" (p. 49). In keeping with the idea of narrative engagement, Hammack and Toolis, drawing especially on Vygotsky's cultural-historical activity theory (CHAT), also seek to emphasize the "situated" and processual nature of narrative and development, in turn, "as a process of ongoing social practice" (p. 52). One prominent instantiation of these ideas may be found in Arnett's (2004) theory of emerging adulthood, which, on Hammack & Toolis's (Chapter 4 of this volume) account, has created new opportunities to study the social, cultural, and historical construction of adulthood. Taking this set of ideas one step further, it can plausibly be argued that Cohler's essay "can be interpreted as a treatise on the social construction of human development" itself, supplying "a blueprint to study the dynamic link between self and society" (p. 53).

Drawing on a quite different tradition of research, McAdams (Chapter 5 of this volume), in his exploration of the life narrative at midlife, also provides compelling support for the "socially constructed" nature of adulthood. I am not sure he would frame his work this way; social constructionism, in its more radical forms especially, would seem to run counter to McAdams's own more "personological" perspective, which is focused especially on "narrative identity," that is, "an internalized and evolving life story that reconstrues the autobiographical past and imagines the future in such a way as to affirm threads of continuity and coherence in a person's life" (Chapter 5, p. 60). On McAdams's account, which draws broadly on Erikson's psychosocial developmental framework, "Stories tell us who we are, who we were, and who we will be. But stories also manage to address more particular problems that may arise at specific points in the life course" (p. 62). For midlife adults, he goes on to suggest, one of the central challenges concerns *generativity*, which entails caring and providing for future generations. In American society, those who are highly generative tend to frame their narratives in terms of redemption: "the protagonist repeatedly encounters setbacks, failures, losses, and disappointments. But negative events are often redeemed by positive outcomes as the protagonist continues to grow and prosper" (p. 63). It is precisely in this distinctively American context that we can begin to discern the social constructionist strain of McAdams's work. For what he shows in this work, compellingly, is that the way in which we construe the stories of our lives is intimately and inextricably bound to the particular societal and cultural surrounds within which we live. "The redemptive stories told by highly generative American adults" thus "evoke powerful metaphors and motifs that run through American culture, history, and heritage" (p. 64). This is not to say that the resultant narratives are mere reflections of such metaphors and motifs. Indeed, as McAdams, following Cohler, notes, "personal narratives do not always line up nicely with the broader stories that may prevail in any given culture and at any particular historical moment" (p. 65). There can be rejection or resistance, an effort to defy the extant canonical script. "Authoring a life story" is therefore "a tricky affair, a psychocultural activity of self-creation and re-creation, operating within the tense and dynamic space that lies between phenomenal experience and cultural reality" (p. 65).

As one might ask at this juncture: To what extent are there constraints upon this construction? More to the point still, to what extent are there constraints upon the process of development itself? It is possible that Cohler himself remained tethered to more traditional ways of thinking about development. As he states in his comments regarding the third developmental transformation, in adulthood, "The first two of the three major life transformations at which there are significant reformulations of the personal narrative are shaped largely by maturational factors, particularly as a result of the development of thought itself. . . . Later, in adulthood," he continues, "maturation plays a much less significant role in development and is largely replaced by subjective assessment of timing and the passage of social milestones in terms of those normatively defined within a particular cohort at a particular historical period" (Cohler, 1982, p. 222). My guess is that Cohler would modify this statement now; even in the earliest years, the relevant formative factors go well beyond the confines of the maturational, the organismic. As we move into adulthood, in any case, we see that these cultural and historical factors loom ever larger.

Cohler himself emerges as something of a "social constructionist" with words like those he offered in this section of the essay. He also cites work by people like Ken Gergen frequently and, by all indications, approvingly. But his is not a purely constructionist account—in part because he is more willing to invoke maturational processes and the like but also because he recognizes that the normativity found across the life course is structured, that there are certain existential realities and "rhythms" that constrain the movement of both life and its reconstruction. In the case of midlife, one such existential reality concerns one's mortality. "The reality of a limited lifetime is increasingly apparent across the middle years," Cohler writes (p. 223). "The death of parents and close friends"—and cherished teachers— "serves as a constant reminder of mortality. However," he adds, "mourning is necessary not only for such losses but also for lost hopes and aspirations" (p. 223). It is as a result of such consciousness "that both duration of time and the relative impact of the remembered past are transformed across midlife in relation to the experienced present and anticipated future" (p. 223). And this consciousness takes form in and through the sociocultural surround, as a function of extant norms and beliefs, values and practices. "Once again," therefore, he writes, "it is important to note the continuing interrelationship between social and developmental factors in determining the nature of the personal narrative across the life course" (p. 224).

We see this relationship once again in Lieblich's chapter (Chapter 6 of this volume) on narrating life after 65. In dialogue both with Cohler's essay and with Robert Butler's (1963) pioneering article *The Life Review: An Interpretation of Reminiscence in the Aged*, Lieblich explores the extent to which the kind of structuration referred to above cut across two quite different populations of individuals she interviewed. She therefore asks: "Are the elderly indeed particularly prone to tell about their past lives as compared to other age groups? How is the inclination to narrate manifested? What may characterize the aged who prefer to tell, or rather not to tell? Is telling beneficial for one's well-being?" (Chapter 6, p. 74). Her answers: Some elders are prone to tell and others not. Of those inclined to tell, there was "deep gratitude for providing them with the opportunity to recount their life and family history" (p. 76), and of those not inclined to do so, there could be outright refusal, the supposition among some being that there really wasn't anything significant to tell and that the past was better left behind. "Thus," Lieblich writes, "the essential difference that emerged between the two studies was that the first group willingly undertook the process of life review because they were able to conceive of their past as serving their values and ideals, or highly meaningful as a historical lesson, while the second group did not share this tendency because they had a hard time finding pride and meaning in their past" (p. 78). The implication: "not all of them are willing to conduct a life review at this stage, nor do they indulge in spontaneous reminiscence" (p. 79). What's more, there was no evidence to suggest that those who engaged in life review were better adjusted than those who didn't. In the end, Lieblich suggests that we look at these two groups as representing different systems of values, along with the different social-historical backgrounds that may have given rise to them, in order to understand the marked disparities at hand.

## Rethinking the Story of Development

Lieblich's perspective on the issues at hand, not unlike those of several others we have examined, points toward a more fluid and variable conception of the life course than Cohler himself had posited. These perspectives also point toward a more fluid and variable conception of *development*. Indeed, what they suggest is that the process of development is itself a kind of narrative, one that must be told and retold ever again, in accordance with the ever-changing sociohistorical circumstances within which individuals live and narrate their lives. We are thus considering two transformational processes, one taking place at the level of the *personal* story and the other taking place at the level of the *developmental* story, that is, the theory of development. As Cohler writes toward the end of his essay, "As a result of such transformations [as we have been considering herein], earlier memories change. Together with the changing context of time and situation, these earlier memories are continually revised so as to maintain a sense of continuity across the life course" (p. 228). As we have seen through the chapters of this volume, the story of development changes as well—so much so, in fact, that one may question whether the concept of development has any meaning at all.

Cohler's transformational shifts may no longer apply in quite the same way as they did back in 1982. This should come as no surprise; people change. Cohler was well aware of this. But through it all, he maintained that some of the revising and revisioning processes individuals engaged in could be understood developmentally, if not for all time, then at least for *this* time, this historical moment. His framework thus provides for the possibility of there existing a kind of template—albeit a mobile template, one that would inevitably change over the course of time and history—that can help us identify what functions and purposes personal narratives might serve in furthering the developmental process. As noted earlier, it has become common to acknowledge that memories and narratives change and that, as such, there is no purely "objective" account to be had. With this in mind, some have gone so far as to suggest that, ultimately, personal narratives are best regarded as fictions, imaginative reconstructions tied to the interests, needs, and wishes of the present. This may be so to some extent. But what Cohler adds to this perspective is the idea that these "fictions" can be linked to specific developmental junctures—which in turn suggests, to me at any rate, that they can still speak something akin to the *truth*. It is not the truth of correspondence to the past "as it was." Nor is it to be regarded as some sort of subjective truth, tied to the story one wants to tell. It is not a narrative truth either, a purely aesthetic truth that's mainly a function of coherence, of how, and how well, it all hangs together. Instead, what Cohler is essentially positing in this piece is what might be termed a *developmental truth*, one that has been informed and constituted by a specific interpretive framework—tied, in this case, to specific developmental junctures and their associated reconstructive processes. It is this framework that can allow us to "get hold" of personal narratives and to see what they are doing developmentally. The nature of these narratives, and the developmental work they perform, is bound to change in line with changing sociohistorical conditions. So too, therefore, will the developmental story that needs to be told. In this respect, Schiff (Chapter 1 of this volume) offers, perhaps Cohler's thinking, along with that which has been put forth by the authors of the chapters in this volume, "will serve as a reference point for psychologists who would like to *re*-think their approach to development through the lens of a narrative perspective that is sensitive to interpretation and context in human lives" (p. 4).

Cohler's perspective is a quite remarkable one, able to accommodate both the constructed nature of personal narratives *and* a vision of the truth that goes beyond the purely subjective. This dual inclusion, in my view, is at the heart not only of interpretive social science, as it pertains to the study of lives, but also of any and all endeavors that see in narrative a vehicle for reimagining and revisioning the very *idea* of science, as it pertains to the human realm. By bringing the idea of narrative to bear on developmental psychology, Cohler has brought a measure of art to the project of science, the stories we tell, as individuals and as developmentalists, serving to make sense and meaning out of the movement of human lives.

This just scratches the surface of his legacy for developmental psychology and for the narrative psychology he helped to inaugurate. There is more there, much more, and we are lucky to have it.

## References

Arnett, J. (2004). *Emerging adulthood: The winding road from the late teens through the twenties*. New York, NY: Oxford University Press.
Bartlett, F. C. (1995). *Remembering: A study in experimental and social psychology*. Cambridge, UK: Cambridge University Press. (Original work published 1932)
Butler, R. (1963). The life review: An interpretation of reminiscence in the aged. *Psychiatry, 26*, 65–76.
Cohler, B. J. (1982). Personal narrative and life course. In P. Baltes & O. G. Brim (Eds.), *Life-span development and behavior* (Vol. 4, pp. 205–241). New York, NY: Academic Press.
Freeman, M. (1984). History, narrative, and life-span developmental knowledge. *Human Development, 27*, 1–19.
Freeman, M. (1991). Rewriting the self: Development as moral practice. In M. B. Tappan & M. J. Packer (Eds.), *New Directions for Child and Adolescent Development: No. 54. Narrative and storytelling: Implications for understanding moral development* (pp. 83–102). San Francisco, CA: Jossey-Bass.

Freeman, M. (1998). Mythical time, historical time, and the narrative fabric of the self. *Narrative Inquiry, 8*, 27–50.

Freeman, M. (2003). Rethinking the fictive, reclaiming the real: Autobiography, narrative time, and the burden of truth. In G. Fireman, T. McVay, & O. Flanagan (Eds.), *Narrative and consciousness: Literature, psychology, and the brain* (pp. 115–128). New York, NY: Oxford University Press.

Freeman, M. (2010a). *Hindsight: The promise and peril of looking backward.* New York, NY: Oxford University Press.

Freeman, M. (2010b). "Even amidst": Rethinking narrative coherence. In M. Hyvarinen, L.-C. Hydén, M. Saarenheimo, & M. Tamboukou (Eds.), *Beyond narrative coherence* (pp. 167–186). Amsterdam, The Netherlands: John Benjamins.

Freud, S. (1960). *Leonardo da Vinci and a memory of his childhood* (Standard Edition, XI, pp. 63–137). London, UK: Hogarth. (Original work published 1910)

Freud, S. (1966). *Project for a scientific psychology* (Standard Edition, I). London, UK: Hogarth. (Original work published 1895)

Gadamer, H.-G. (1975). *Truth and method.* New York, NY: Crossroads.

Ricoeur, P. (1984). *Time and narrative* (Vol. 1). Chicago, IL: University of Chicago Press.

Ross, B. M. (1991). *Remembering the personal past.* New York, NY: Oxford University Press.

Ross, B. M., & Wilson, A. E. (2000). Constructing and appraising past selves. In D. L. Schacter & E. Scarry (Eds.), *Memory, brain, and belief* (pp. 231–258). Cambridge, MA: Harvard University Press.

Shils, E. (1981). *Tradition.* Chicago, IL: University of Chicago Press.

MARK FREEMAN *is a professor and the chair of the Department of Psychology and distinguished professor of ethics and society at the College of the Holy Cross.*

NEW DIRECTIONS FOR CHILD AND ADOLESCENT DEVELOPMENT • DOI: 10.1002/cad

# INDEX